MUST
EAT

AMSTERDAM

MUST EAT

EAT

AMSTERDAM

AN ECLECTIC SELECTION OF CULINARY LOCATIONS

LUC HOORNAERT
PHOTOGRAPHY: KRIS VLEGELS

LANNOO

CONTENTS

€: UNDER € 12,5 • €€: € 12,5 - 25 • €€€: € 25 - 40 • €€€€: OVER € 40

Average price for a regular main dish and a drink.

CENTRE - 6

SEA PALACE

Oosterdokskade 8 - 1011 AE Amsterdam
T +31 20 626 4777 - www.seapalace.nl
Mon.-Sun. 12.00-23.00, dim sum served Mon.-Sun. 12.00-16.00

Many people who visit Amsterdam know the spectacular Sea Palace, in fact you can't miss it. With its 700 seats, it is the largest restaurant in Amsterdam, and the first floating restaurant in Europe.

one of the most popular examples from the dim sum repertoire

Siu mai

Therefore, it has everything to do with a tourist trap, but don't judge a book by its cover! Under the striking green lacquered roof is one of the best Chinese restaurants this side of the world.

Dim sum is my absolute favorite way to eat. I am always highly impressed by the speed at which genuine dim sum restaurants are able to serve an unbelievable variety of flavors and shapes. All guests sample and enjoy; the atmosphere is super pleasant and everyone finds what he loves, and loves what he finds.

Dim sum is not—as many people mistakenly believe—a specific appetizer. It refers to a manner of eating. Dim sum literally means 'touch the heart'. In Cantonese, it is called yum cha, which actually means 'to drink tea'. This better uncovers the origin of dim sum. It comes from the era of the Silk Road when many resting places were built for travelers; tea was served with small snacks. Many of my heroic meals were dim sum meals.

Siu mai or shumai, or pork dumplings, is one of the most popular examples from the dim sum repertoire. The Cantonese version is the one that deserves the most fame. In southeast Guangdong, a siu mai usually consists of pork meat, chopped shrimp, black mushrooms, spring onion, ginger, and a little soy sauce, shaoxing (Chinese rice wine), sesame oil, and chicken stock. This mixture is skillfully rolled in a sheet of dough, then steamed and generally topped with a colorful accent.

Most likely, siu mai first appeared in the Mongolian inland, in Huhhot to be more precise, sometime between the Ming and Qing dynasties. The dish was reserved for refined tea houses before being brought by merchants from the Chinese province of Shanxi to Beijing and the port city of Tianjin. From this moment, the spread became explosive and this bomb of flavor thrived everywhere in culinary China.

Rightfully so, a well-prepared siu mai is one of the very best bites you can ever put in your mouth. A siu mai is so flavorful that its bite is addictive; it is a sort of 'kick' that otherwise you can only find in the best of the best frankfurter. To ideally enjoy the mouth feel, you should put the entire siu mai in your mouth at once so that your taste buds are put to work and the mouth feel becomes an essential part of the tasting experience.

Dim Ergo Sum!

MAE SOMJAJ

Koningsstraat 25 - 1011 ET Amsterdam
T +31 6 511 75 049 - www.maesomjai.com
Tue.-Sun. 12.00-21.00

Thai food is one of the most widely appreciated foods in the world. It is a perfect fusion of its neighbouring regions, India and China. This results in complex flavours, which please many palates.

Laab Kai

a real Thai experience

Thai chefs work hard to balance all the flavours and influences they put into a dish, and this is not an easy task, especially for someone who is not from Thailand. Thai food charms with its freshness and subtle spiciness, and is mostly composed of healthy ingredients.

Often with gastronomical cultures, a lot of focus gets lost once the food crosses the border, and Thai food is no exception, so that eating at a Thai place in Holland is rarely an exciting experience. Luckily, however there are exceptions, such as this small, humble place in the Koningsstraat.

The restaurant is filled with objects and pictures that remind the guests and the owners of home. A lot of Thai people eat here which, in my opinion, is a good sign, especially in terms of authenticity and taste. The kitchen staff is women only, and I've rarely seen more dedication and focus than in this tiny kitchen. All the sauces and dips are made to order using a mortar and pestle to obtain exactly the right texture. In an era of hi-tech kitchen equipment, this is a real statement. A second statement is the restaurant's refusal to adapt Thai flavours to the Western palate.

Mae Somjaj is proud of her Thai dishes and when eating here you definitely understand why. Don't come here if you're in a hurry because at Mae Somjaj everything is made from scratch. No fast-food versions of Thai classics, but precision and depth of flavour. The ever-popular Laab Kai, or spicy minced chicken salad, is a real stunner and has a balance close to perfection. Balance is, in fact, the key word at Mae Somjaj.

Your taste buds will never forgive you if you don't go for the authentic Thai experience in this humble grand eatery.

Restaurant Gebr. Hartering

GEBROEDERS HARTERING

Peperstraat 10hs - 1011 TL Amsterdam
T +31 20 421 0699 - www.gebrhartering.nl
Tue.-Wed. 18.00-22.30, Thu.-Sat. 18.00-23.00, Sun. 18.00-22.00

Paul and Niek Hartering are an Amsterdam sensation with their Burgundy cuisine. I feel like I'm eating at the Hartering's home rather than at their restaurant. Exactly like a French table d'hôtes: you eat what they serve. There is no fixed menu, except for the Fleckvieh rib.

Fleckvieh rib

However, the menu changes every day and is timely posted on the website. There is always a crowd, hence some chaos. I actually enjoy this bustle; the dishes served here shine with simplicity and flavor. They added a somewhat improvised dining room with a few seats in the basement, and in the summer, they have a floating terrace-boat where guests can enjoy the water. It is actually a fun place because every time a small boat sails by all the tables and glasses start wavering.

The two 'brothers in arms' do not dream of perfectly clothed tables covered in crystal and silver; their greatest attention goes to their guests. Is everything to their taste? The crisis led them to reflect on an alternative to filling plates with expensive, luxurious ingredients.

The principle of 'sharing' is used here in a very unique way and I have seldom seen a restaurant of such high culinary level where dishes are shared between tables. The fixed menu is displayed in common dishes in the middle of the table so that everyone can eat as much as they want. In Amsterdam, these preparations are what they call 'nouveau-ruig' (nouveau rough). For me, these are dishes created by two experts who serve the food that they love. Informal, laid-back, but

always professional. The brothers are not comfortable in a five-star setting or with the mandatory fuss that goes with it. Their foundation is their craft. Their uncle was a butcher and their father was a carpenter—talk about two traditional trades! They are not innovators, and I find their refreshing lack of creativity a very positive and seminal characteristic; as a matter of fact, many restaurant owners have been inspired by this no-nonsense approach. Also, nothing is thrown away. This is the only restaurant I know that makes, for example, various fish sauces using fish heads. Sometimes, the work of the Hartering brothers is very similar to that of a missionary. It is amazing how many guests have never eaten offal and literally have to be won over.

In this restaurant, they like to work with a charcoal grill, because it symbolizes a return to the roots. Their only signature dish is the Fleckvieh rib. This cow breed was isolated in 1830 when Simmental cows were exported from Switzerland to Bavaria and Austria to improve local breeds. The result is a breed that is stable and more robust than the Holstein while still producing the same quality of milk. The meat has a deep taste and texture and a nice proportion of fat, as is the case for the Holstein

VERMEER

Prins Hendrikkade 59-72 - 1012 AD Amsterdam
T + 31 20 556 4885 - www.restaurantvermeer.nl
Mon.-Sat. 18.30-22.00

Passion and ambition are the key words defining the art of Chris Naylor, the chef at this phenomenal fine dining restaurant just steps away from Central Station.

Tasting menu

Naylor is British and has been running the Vermeer kitchen since 2004. Vermeer is a part of the 5-star NH Collection Barbizon Palace hotel.

Naylor tries to use only local ingredients, and whenever he can he buys from local growers just minutes outside the city. Herbs are grown and harvested on top of the adjacent NH Collection Barbizon Palace. Naylor learned to cook in Cheshire, United Kingdom, at Weaverham High School and Mid-Cheshire College of Further Education. In the Netherlands, he started as sous-chef in Hotel Grand under Albert Roux. Later, he moved to La Rive and worked as junior sous-chef under Robert Kranenborg. He continued to collaborate with Kranenborg as sous-chef in Vossius and head-chef in Le Cirque.

His cooking style is very green, meaning he gives preference to vegetables when creating dishes. This is one of the reasons his food gurus are Michel Bras and Alice Waters. He also advocates a deeper understanding of British cuisine (which I fully support and agree with). Too few people understand the importance of British cuisine and its influence on contemporary cuisine trends throughout Europe and perhaps beyond.

Naylor's dishes highlight the real essence of cooking. He uses few ingredients and his talent lies in pairing them to create exciting dishes. Naylor is a true class act, rewarded with a Michelin star.

TAKA JAPANESE KITCHEN

Stormsteeg 9 - 1012 BD Amsterdam
T + 31 6 261 75939 - www.facebook.com/ayanokouji.sasuke
Wed.-Sat. 12.00-15.00, Sun. 12.30-15.00

Imagine an oriental food store with a secret. Well, Toko Dun Yong is keeping a fantastic secret from you. No signs, no menus, nothing whatsoever, but on the second floor you step inside the world of Taka Kito, a modest but very talented chef from Tokyo with a mission.

Spicy miso ramen

Every week he designs new ads that make fun of McDonald's or some other fast-food icon. These ads, which praise his own fast food and appear on his Facebook page, are the only clue you get to discover this little gem.

The restaurant looks more like a living room. There's a stove surrounded by five tables, walls filled with artworks for sale, some fake plants, and a lot of delicious Japanese street food. Born and raised in Tokyo, Kito trained as an accounting manager. In 2008, he came to Holland on a business trip and worked here for a year. The first thing he noticed was a serious lack of healthy, decent, tasty street food. Most of the stuff was crammed with sugar and there wasn't much choice. The only quality food was in expensive restaurants that young people couldn't afford for their daily lunches. In Japan, you can eat great and healthy food on every street corner for just a few euros.

He somehow knew that he had the potential to be a good chef. He loved good food, but he was a little lazy when it came to preparing it. Nevertheless, he set his mind to it and went to a cooking school in Tokyo for four years before deciding to return to Holland and open a healthy-street-food restaurant.

First, however, he worked in a traditional Japanese izakaya in Tokyo that had no Michelin stars but served hearty Japanese bistrot food. His first experiments in Holland with small Japanese dishes didn't work out because Dutch people prefer one big portion to five smaller ones. So he started making his own noodle soup and a kind of noodle pancake with cabbage, kimchee, beef, fish, and crab.

His dishes are simply delicious and take you right to the heart of Japan. Tasty soul food, all home-made by a chef who has both feet on the ground. He's quite happy running a small restaurant with happy guests that love his food. He doesn't want a bigger place and has found his niche on the second floor of a food store in the Amsterdam Chinese district. He works eight hours a day, spends some time on his hobby, and sleeps for eight hours. This balance makes him a content and successful chef.

I really love this place.

BORD'EAU

BORD'EAU
HOTEL DE L'EUROPE

Nieuwe Doelenstraat 2-14 - 1012 CP Amsterdam
T +31 20 531 1705 - www.bordeau.nl
lunch Tue.-Fri. 12.00-14.30, dinner Tue.-Sat. 18.30-22.30

Hotel de l'Europe is one of the most iconic and beautiful hotels in Amsterdam. It is right on the banks of the Amstel River that gives this beautiful city its name. Although the building was transformed into a luxury hotel in 1896, we can trace its history back further.

Green apple, walnut, caramel

It lies on the foundations of the Rondeel Tower that was constructed as part of the city's defense in 1535. In 1638 an inn was built here, and in 1772 a newspaper article referred to the inn as 'Wapen v Amsterdam'. Heineken purchased it in 2008 and transformed it into the phenomenal place it is today.

In 1940, the Hotel de l'Europe made its film debut in Hitchcock's *Foreign Correspondent*. It was used as a location for the film and we can actually see dear old Alfred doing one of his famous cameo's as he walks past the hotel reading a newspaper. In another scene of the film we can see partially defective lights on the roof reading Hot Europe, which was a reference to the political situation in Europe, when the hotel was occupied by German officers during the war.

However, we are particularly interested in their flagship restaurant, Bord'eau, a haven of tranquility. The executive chef and creative mind behind it is Richard Van Oostenbrugge who traded in his role as chef at Envy to oversee

the contemporary creative cuisine in this multi-Michelin starred restaurant. Richard took along his Envy sous-chef, Thomas De Groot. These two teamed up with one of the biggest Dutch culinary icons, Robert Kranenborgh.

Together, they oversee a young and ambitious team serving attractive, refined, creative contemporary food, always backed up by extensive knowledge of the classic French cuisine repertoire. The food is prepared with great precision and distinction. Flavor combinations are more than interesting. This young team, guided by classical masters, provides an impressive balance between classic technique and contemporary style. Of course, choosing a Must Eat here is somewhat disrespectful to the laws of gastronomy. Nonetheless, the apple creation is highly ingenious and illustrates the potential of this restaurant. As a child everybody was fond of these love apples, coated with crackling sugar. This is a contemporary version of the childhood classic and it also reminds me of Adam and Eve's forbidden apple.

TON TON CLUB

Sint Annendwarsstraat 6 - 1012 HC Amsterdam
T +31 20 261 89 24 - www.tontonclub.nl
Mon.-Tue. 17.00-23.00, Wed.-Sun. 11.00-23.00, kitchen opens at 17.00

Serdar is very passionate about good food and about old school arcades.
Inspired by the Williamsburg Barcade, where the original arcade opened
in 2004 in a former metal shop, he opened the Ton Ton club in the red
light district.

Bloodhound, applesauce, onions, chives and mustard

a pitch-black dog, somewhere between a blood sausage and a classic hot dog

It is a unique combination of vintage arcade games, rare high quality craft beers and damn good creative hotdogs.

It is in fact the long lost arcade that Amsterdam never had, and in this area where the focus is on pleasure, the Ton Ton club feels like a good fit. The location is in a very narrow street in the beating heart of the red light district, right behind 'de Oude Kerk', the oldest existing building in Amsterdam. It was founded in 1213 and consecrated in 1306 by the Bishop of Utrecht with Saint Nicolas as its patron saint. It has been a Calvinist church since the Reformation in 1578.

A specialty here is the Bloodhound: a pitch-black dog, somewhere between a blood sausage and a classic hot dog. It is a specialty dog made by the guys at Brandt & Levie. By replacing reduced pork broth with pig's blood, they obtain this unique black dog with a classical Frankfurter-bite to it. Applesauce complements it beautifully. Applesauce and blood sausage are indeed one of my childhood memories of delicious home-made cooking.

Spending an afternoon at Ton Ton is good fun. You can ruthlessly kick your friend's ass at Mortal Kombat or just chill here with a great beer and an even better hotdog. The Dogs they make at Brandt & Levie are so far out that they inspire me to change the lyrics of *D2B*, a rap classic from Problem's 2012 album, *Welcome to Mollywood,* where in the intro a female rapper can't leave her boyfriend because of a real case of D2B (Dick Too Bomb). These dogs are D2B, Dog too Bomb.

It has this old-school vibe that makes it irresistible and timeless. See you soon at Ton Ton!

ANNA

Warmoesstraat 111 - 1012 JA Amsterdam
T + 31 20 428 1111 - www.restaurantanna.nl
Open daily, 17.00 till late night

Anna is one of the few great eateries in Amsterdam's Red Light District,
located in the heart of the oldest part of the city.

Slow-cooked veal cheek, crispy salsify, mashed celeriac, pumpkin seeds

During the Reformation in the 16th century, several monasteries in the old centre were shut down. The old churches were reformed and the Christianity's entire expression changed, but Saint Anna persevered. And she was immortalised in Amsterdam via Sint-Annenstraat and Sint-Annendwarsstraat. And off course, since 2011, as Restaurant Anna.

Anna was actually Jesus' grandmother, but the Bible doesn't even care to mention Maria's mother. During the Middle Ages, she became an important saint who is usually depicted with her daughter and grandson as 'Anna te Drieën'. Anna became the patron saint of carpenters, tailors, pregnant women, and bachelors looking for a partner.

Since Anna opened in 2011, they fill a special place in the Red Light District. When Lodewijk Asscher, former mayor of the city, decided to upgrade the Red Light District, Anna's team didn't miss the boat. They were the first contemporary bistro in the area and the first place in Amsterdam to use iPads. A few weeks after the opening they got a raving review from legendary Dutch food critic Johannes Van Dam, and the quality of the food hasn't changed since. Even better, Anna recently attracted Chef Ben Van Geelen, former owner of A La Ferme, who is running the kitchen now and doing a splendid job. He's putting even more authenticity and terroir into the dishes, and that is a comforting thought.

Anna is still going strong, very strong.

KAAGMAN EN KORTEKAAS

Sint Nicolaasstraat 43 - 1012 NJ Amsterdam
T + 31 20 233 6544 - www.kaagmanenkortekaas.nl
Thu.-Sat. 18.00-22.30

Friends Bram and Giel proved that you can open a restaurant in the centre
of Amsterdam and turn it into an overnight success. Both partners are
bursting with talent. Bram takes care of the guests and Giel is the chef.

Daily changing menu

Besides being a great and talented chef, Giel is also a true artisan. He's been working in kitchens in Belgium and Holland since he was 12. His two main sources of inspiration in Amsterdam are the top-notch Italian restaurant Toscanini and Will Demandt of the iconic Bordewijk restaurant, where he was a chef for many years.

Giel has an insatiable hunger for knowledge about artisan gastronomy and has become a great all-round chef. He excels at making charcuterie (cold meat) and is truly great at adding the excitement factor to simple, informal dishes. He transforms simple, everyday dishes into real gastronomical delights. The experience he gained at Toscanini taught him to keep dishes overall natural, without fancy frills, and no nonsense—the Italian way.

Reading through the menu at Kaagman & Kortekaas, it's hard to make a choice: every dish looks tasty and tempting. Giel's cooking is refined but raw, enticing, and teasing, with a lot of feeling for precision and elegance. He's one of those chefs who is happy enough to have found his own language, his own style, and who always has one of his two guardian angels looking over his shoulder. He will never copy Toscanini or Will Demandt, but he will use their wisdom to season his own creations. His cuisine is the ultimate combination of contemporary raw cuisine and artisan classic.

GARTINE

Taksteeg 7 - 1012 PB Amsterdam
T + 31 20 320 4132 - www.gartine.nl
Wed.-Sat. 10.00-18.00

Enjoy breakfast, lunch, or high tea in this oasis in the bustling centre of Amsterdam. Gartine—an ancient French word for small pasture—is a small gem, tucked away deeply between shopping streets.

Fennel-olive cake with savory cream cheese, herb salad and olive oil

This tiny place is cosy and romantic, with a focus on vegetables, all home-grown in the owners' own garden outside the city.

The overall ambiance is superfriendly and quietly charming. I don't know why, but the song *It's oh so quiet* by Björk always comes to mind when I think about Gartine. Softly lit and decorated with matching antiques and curios, it's a great place for a girly lunch or a first date. Dishes are served on nice china with assorted cutlery.

Everything here is prepared with love: the slow-food-style breakfast, the heavenly chocolate tarte, and of course, the inevitable fruits, vegetables, and herbs from the garden. Lunch includes unique custom-made sandwiches, soups, and of course a lot of vegetables. Owners Kirstem Eckhart and Willem-Jan Hendriks take their gardening very seriously. They cultivate 1,500 square meters of land, just enough to provide for their restaurant. Even the flowers on the tables come from their garden.

They want to keep the restaurant small—it only accommodates 24 guests—so as to have time to grow their vegetables and fruit. This wonderful restaurant is one of the most intimate places in Amsterdam.

BAK

Van Diemenstraat 410 - 1013 CR Amsterdam
T +31 20 737 2553 - www.bakrestaurant.nl
lunch Wed.-Sun. 11.00-23.00, dinner Wed.-Sun. 18.30-23.00

I don't like pop-up restaurants! Usually, there is a serious catch and the temporary character of a pop-up is precisely the reason not to be good enough. All that under the motto: it is temporary, so we don't have a long term vision for it.

Salt-crusted celeriac, apple and coffee

Except of course when it comes to the check, which in most cases is much higher than at other, more professionally designed initiatives, generally called restaurants.

Of course, there are exceptions. After the three young creators of Bak had spent a few years successfully opening pop-up restaurants in various areas of Amsterdam, they took the leap and opened a fixed location in the Veem building on IJ bay. What began as a weekend experiment eventually turned into a permanent restaurant. Officially, they were allowed to remain at that location for one year; however something tells me that a solution to this problem will come up one way or another.

Bak found its venue in Het Veem, an old warehouse in the Oude Houthaven (the old lumber haven), where coffee, tea and tobacco were once stored. Bak is located on the fourth floor of this warehouse. It has an inspiring decor, all in the spirit of the times. The inte-

rior and atmosphere are somewhat rough and wild, and by that I mean second-hand café furniture arranged in a very white backdrop. Through two gigantic windows and a few smaller openings, you have a delightful view over part of the Amsterdam harbour.

The whole is really beautiful and I like to talk of a Bak experience. This experience is certainly enriched by the young people who perfectly complete the creative, sometimes rugged dishes from the kitchen. The girls wearing a black apron with trendy leggings, and the boys in necktie pamper their guests.

The laid-back atmosphere that reigns here is unique. This is exactly why I cannot believe that this restaurant could disappear after a year.

Since the menu changes every day, choosing a 'must eat' is an impossible task. I will leave my gastronomic fate in the expert hands of this unique restaurant.

MARIUS

Barentszstraat 173 - 1013 NM Amsterdam
T +31 20 422 7880 - www.deworst.nl/restaurant-marius-table-dhote/
Closed on Monday & Sunday

In a former life I worked for the iconoclastic, brilliant Randall Grahm,
Rhone Ranger and founder/president for life of Bonny Doon Vineyard,
located in Santa Cruz, CA.

Vitello Tonnato

In the mid-eighties, he was wowing everybody with his winemaking skills to transform ugly duckling grape varietals into super sexy wines. Two of the places where I most enjoy the quintessence of Californian cuisine are The French Laundry and Chez Panisse, the popular restaurant of Alice Waters. Her meals helped me develop my fascination for real food and essential flavours.

When visiting Marius, a homely table d'hôte style restaurant with checkered tablecloths and open kitchen serving a market-driven four-course menu, I couldn't help noticing an impressive amount of books focusing on either La Waters or her iconic restaurant in Berkeley. We started talking to Kees Elfring who worked at Chez Panisse while I was slaving in Randall's winery. We didn't meet in those days but, since I don't believe in coincidences, we were meant to meet. Marius is located on Prinseneiland, which is a group of man-made islands north of the Jordaan neighbourhood and not a location popular with tourists. With only a handful of tables, this place evokes the feeling of a friend's dining room. He was clearly intrigued and inspired by Alice's ground-breaking restaurant. He needs to go to market almost on a daily basis because Kees finds it much easier to visualise a menu when strol-

ling a market. It sure is easier than sitting with his sous-chefs over a couple of beers and a scary, empty piece of paper.

Don't let the cosiness of this restaurant fool you. Kees means serious business and is a kick ass chef. He has this typical cool and laidback style (or am I just imagining this, knowing his background?) of California natives and doesn't believe in the reign of terror most chefs practice in their kitchen. He's a strong believer in the finesse and refinement of simplicity. He doesn't always want to take it a step further to try to show off a little more than his neighbour. Size doesn't matter here. He shares the same idealistic views as Chef Waters.

The eternal, intellectual, and passionate-about-food bond between Alice and Kees come truly come together in the name of both restaurants. Honoré Panisse is one of the main characters in the Marseille based trilogy written by Pagnol. In the story, Marius impregnates Fanny, who has to marry a more prosperous salesman in the harbour of Marseille, Honoré Panisse. However, months after the marriage and the birth of their love child, Marius returns to win back Fanny.

Alice can be very proud of her pupil...

WORST

Barentszstraat 171 - 1013 NM Amsterdam
T +31 20 625 6167 - www.deworst.nl
Tue.-Sat. 12.00-24.00, Sun. 10.00-22.00

Damn! A real Cuban sandwich! It's been a while, and it tastes like… great memories! It is hard to find a great Cuban chef outside certain states in the US, but Kees has nailed it. At Worst, or Marius next door as I like to call it, such things are possible: it is a stage for artisan charcutiers, like Kees himself.

Cuban sandwich

It is hard to determine exactly when the Cuban sandwich originated. It is a variation of a ham and cheese sandwich that was made for Cuban workers in Key West and Ybor City, where the first Cuban immigrant communities in Florida settled. It was later brought to Miami by Cuban exiles and expats. The sandwich is traditionally made with ham, roasted pork, Swiss cheese, pickles, mustard and Cuban bread. The Cuban mix or Cubano's origin is certainly intriguing. In the late 1800s and early 1900s, travelling back and forth between Key West and Tampa was easy, so Cubans frequently sailed back and forth for employment, pleasure and family visits. Nowadays, the world's epicentre for the popular Cubano mixto sandwich is Tampa.

Worst is a brilliant place. Although Marius bears the imprint of the influential establishment where Kees found the chef within him that evolved over the years, Worst proves that he is part of the new breed or new generation of Dutch chefs. These new kids on the block try to develop an appreciation for their country's gastronomic cultural heritage and they share the commitment to high quality local and traditional produce. The preparations here are simple so the full flavour and potential of the superb cheeses and charcuterie easily speak for themselves. Kees shows his international awareness of how to treat his national larder.

Essentially, this is a great wine bar with an emphasis on extraordinary charcuterie and dishes that require minimum intervention to pair with your chosen bottles. Some of the charcuterie is homemade; the rest comes from artisan local producers who will definitely blow you away, quality wise. This hidden little gem really merits all your attention.

Worst is a very relaxed, laidback, cosy place. It always reminds me of the perfect imaginary butcher shop south of the 45th parallel where the food always seems to taste better. Here, they only serve food where charcuterie lovers have a smile on their face. There are simply too many options. My favourite is the sexy blood sausage made by Floris and Diny from de Pasteibakkerij. But then for reasons of colour contrast only, you need to go for the Veal Weisswurst from Munich, which comes with a dollop of mustard. The occasional Bremer Pinkel is a real treat and is served with sauerkraut and mash. The extraordinary pig's trotter from the reputed Girardeau in Saumur is a real delicacy, especially with white beans and bell peppers. But the Cuban with Tinjethaler cheese is hard to beat. Tinjethaler is a cheese from Friesland elaborated with the same bacteria that gives Emmenthaler its typical taste.

Don't let the name fool you. At worst you are guaranteed a quality-driven night out.

T-Bone

1385
1495
1685
1800

SPINGAREN

Herengracht 88 - 1015 BS Amsterdam
T +31 20 624 9635 - www.spingaren.nl
Mon.-Fri. 17.30-22.30

Pastrami is like a journey in time. The term signifies an age-old method of preserving meat by pickling, drying it slightly, mixing it with various herbs and then slowly smoking and steaming it.

PASTRAMI

pickling, drying, mixing, smoking and steaming

New Amsterdam Pastrami

Pastrami's origins are not entirely clear. It might have originated in Turkey where it was called *pastirma* or perhaps in Romania where *pastra* means 'to store'. We will never be quite sure. What is for certain is that the first pastrami sandwiches emerged in NY during the wave of Jewish immigration from Romania and Bessarabia. In Yiddish it was called *pastrome,* which evolved into *pastrama* in English and later, analogous to salami, it became *pastrami.* Katz's Deli on East Houston in NYC made Pastrami immortal ever since.

I came across Spingaren and their heavenly pastrami sandwich at Rollende Keukens, the mother of all Dutch Food festivals. Spingaren is going brick-and-mortar and they have the only charcuterie (cold cuts) restaurant in the city. Everything here is home made, and if you can't live without it, you can take some home with you. Spingaren is a gorgeous restaurant that glorifies the noble art of preserving meat, turning it into heavenly charcuterie for you to sample, taste and devour. A place you will like, love and cherish.

DE KLEPEL

Prinsenstraat 22 - 1015 DD Amsterdam
T +31 20 623 8244 - www.cafedeklepel.nl
Mon.-Fri. open at 18.00, Sat.-Sun. open at 16.00

Cafe De Klepel is all about wine! Everything here breathes wine.
At De Klepel, they have a tremendous wine list, and of course, if you
drink great wine, you might as well eat great food with it.

Food to match great wine

This used to be a dive, but it has been pimped into a very elegant although simple boutique restaurant where great wine and food rule. It reminds me of the imaginary perfect wine restaurant in France. The kind of place you dream about if you are an epicurean like I am. The place is so inviting, so picture perfect, that it seems to be reaching out to you and saying: Please come in and fall in love with me.

All this is done in a very natural, nononsense style. No marketing, just plain honesty and authenticity with a capital A. You can fit the entire concept or better, raison d'être of De Klepel into just one picture. Wine, great cheese, fantastic bread and charcuterie, some canned miracles... Everyone who loves food will agree that that is all you need to be happy.

I really love the idea of essential simplicity. It's like if an artist needs two pages to explain his work, he missed the point. A masterpiece has this unmistakable ability to strike you, and that is exactly what De Klepel does. Margot Los, the talented young sommelier, is really passionate about wine and food. Together with chefs Maarten Van Pinksteren and the Belgium trained Pieter, they concoct dishes and try to find perfect cheeses, charcuterie and, why not, canned vintage sardines that are complimentary to great wines. Also, a plethora of simple, humble preparations bursting with flavor, prepared daily.

A brilliant, under the radar hot spot for locals you are bound to fall in love with. It is destiny!

TOSCANINI

Lindengracht 75 - 1015 KD Amsterdam
T +31 20 623 2813 - www.restauranttoscanini.nl
Mon.-Sat. 18.00 -22.30

In 1985, a restaurant with a large, luminous space and an open kitchen opened its doors in the Jordaan district. Since its opening, Toscanini has been the norm, the benchmark for delicious Italian cuisine in Amsterdam and maybe even in the Netherlands.

Ravioli di ricotta e peperoni al nero di seppia, polpo alla brace

Here reigns a sort of happy chaos, probably familiar to all Italians. It often happens that a restaurant will be created out of love for simple, fresh Italian cuisine that everybody loves. A good Italian chef is a wizard, capable of preparing a full, gastronomic meal with very few ingredients. This love, dedication, and passion are still here. As should be the case in any great Italian restaurant, everything here is prepared on-site. At Toscanini they rely on the power of Italian cuisine in all its simplicity and sincerity. All vegetables are brought in directly from Italy; pasta and bread are made in-house.

Leonardo Pacenti, the Italian-Dutch wonder child, was born in South Africa and lived there until he was 11. He came with his parents to the Netherlands and subsequently moved to Rome, where he went to work in restaurants to pay for his education. It appears he found his passion: cooking. When a friend launched Toscanini and asked Leonardo to participate, he didn't hesitate for a second.

Authentic food and a pleasant atmosphere: that does it!

In Italy, I have never eaten one bad meal; consequently, selecting a 'must eat' is a difficult task in this case. I have a preference for Toscanini's fish dishes. The ravioli stuffed with ricotta and paprika, served with a rich sauce of squid and squid ink is an excellent example. A perfect fusion of balance and flavor produce a very nice dish. On Lindengracht by the two white lanterns, you must go when you want to feel like you're in Italy.

DAALDER

Lindengracht 90 - 1015 KK Amsterdam
T +31 20 624 8864 - www.daalderamsterdam.nl
lunch daily from 12.00-14.00, Sat. 10.00-15.30, dinner daily from 18.00-22.00

Daalder is a gastropub. This means that they serve high quality food in a
pub-like setting. Daalder is set in the Jordaan district, which was originally
a working class neighborhood that grew into one of the most upscale
locations in the city.

Tasting menu

Apparently, the name was derived from the French word for garden, *jardin*, because of the impressive quantity of flowers and trees present. But it seems more that the local nickname for the Prinsengracht canal, the Jordaan, which is in fact the local name for the Jordan River, gave its name to this wonderful part of town. Rembrandt van Rijn spent his last years in this neighborhood, on the Rozengracht Canal to be precise. He is buried in the Westerkerk, at the corner of Rozengracht and Prinsengracht, just beyond the Jordaan. The house where Anne Frank went into hiding during WW II is located on the Prinsengracht, on the outskirts of the Jordaan.

Markets are held regularly in the Jordaan, and also on Lindengracht, where Daalder is located. The restaurant's founder Remco Daalder, didn't have to contemplate long before finding a name for his place. One of the slogans to attract people to the market used to be: 'on the market, your guilder is worth a daalder'. The Dutch guilder was the currency of Holland before the Euro, and a daalder was 2,5 guilder. This, as well as Daadler being Remco's surname, made it an apt name for the place. Daalder was born.

Daalder's gastronomical ambitions are high. And to that end, they have a to-notch contemporary chef in their tiny kitchen. Dennis Huwae used to be at the helm of the famous &samhoud places, where he and head chef Moshik Roth received two Michelin stars for their restaurant. Dennis is a highly driven and talented young chef who consistently delivers precise and outstanding work. Dennis co-owns Daalder, and his style of cuisine is often described as spontaneously created works of art, small gems reflecting vision. His style of cuisine is usually served in a more formal setting, but at Daalder the vibe is relaxed. A unique combo

Have you ever eaten from a wooden floor that the Queen walked on? Here's your chance! The counter at Daalder was made from the original wooden floor of the iconic Rijksmuseum. Eating at Daalder is already high on every foodie's list. The no-nonsense philosophy executed to perfection by current owners Frans van Dam and Wilke Durand is paying off. There is of course the vintage interior which is an anachronism compared to the contemporary dishes, but it works beautifully. Food is the most important part of this restaurant.

NEVER TRUST
A
SKINNY COOK

BORDEWIJK

Noordermarkt 7 - 1015 MV Amsterdam
T +31 20 624 3899 - www.bordewijk.nl
Tue.-Sat. 18.30-22.30

Wil Demandt is an autodidact. He studied history because he wanted to mean something for humanity. However, after a few years, he knew that these studies wouldn't do it.

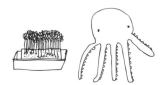

Sepia, langoustine, house-made blood sausage, ink sauce, watercress salad with pecorino

Since he didn't want to end up a frustrated teacher, he resolutely chose his other great passion: cooking. His mother was not a great cook, so he had to learn by himself. He acquired the finesse by observing carefully and listening to the right people. Wil Demandt has been at work for about 32 years, of which 29 years were spent at the Bordewijk restaurant. Many chefs see him as their hero.

His restaurant, with a sophisticated interior, was one of the first bistros in Amsterdam. This is why Bordewijk immediately became the talk of the town. Since its opening, the restaurant has grown into a staple, far beyond Amsterdam. Wil Demandt only uses regional products from responsible farms, fish from day-fishermen, respectfully fed animals, seasonal wild game, superior cheeses and carefully selected wines.

Enter inside Wil's world, the world of suckling piglets and chitterlings, all transformed into delicatessen with craftsmanship and inspiration. Bordewijk is considered one of the very best French restaurants in the Netherlands; this is where Wil cooks classic French tradition for his fans. His prices are very reasonable. His clients are mostly locals who rave over the unique atmosphere in this minimalist restaurant.

This is truly a hidden jewel and the best kept secret of a low-profile address in Amsterdam.

LA PERLA

Tweede Tuindwarsstraat 53 - 1015 RZ Amsterdam
T +31 20 624 8828 - www.pizzaperla.nl
Sun.-Thu. 12.00-22.00, Fri.-Sat. 12.00-22.30

Good pizza is hard to find in Amsterdam, but no worries. Right in the centre of Amsterdam's Jordaan area you will find this small yet bustling street generally referred to as Little Italy. An impressive number of Italian restaurants offer an array of Italian specialities but only one specializes in phenomenal pizza.

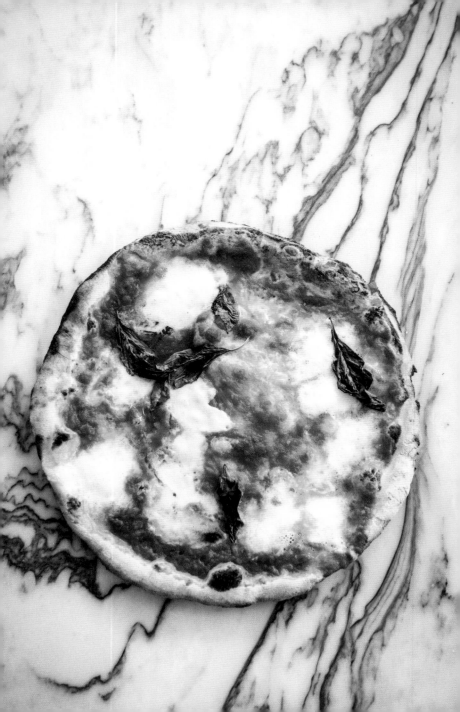

Pizza Margherita

La Perla is actually two restaurants on opposite sides of the street: one focuses exclusively on the art of making pizza and across the street you can enjoy this pizza and also other Italian delicacies. They also have an impressive Italian wine list.

All the produce at La Perla is imported from Italy on a weekly basis, the only way to make pizza that will give you a feeling of Italy. In the middle of the restaurant is a large, wood-fired, brick oven. This is essential for making good pizza, the ultimate comfort food.

One of the darkest days in Italian culinary history must have been when Sam Panapoulos became the first person to put pineapple (from a can) on a pizza base, thereby inventing the Hawaiian Pizza. This dreadful event took place in 1962 in Ontario, Canada, where the Greek ran a pizza joint. Yet, thanks to the tourists, pizza Hawaii is the most popular pizza in Italy. It has been suggested that pizza originated as a plate in the area of the Mediterranean Sea; people would bake flat bread and use it as a plate on which they put their food. If someone had an extremely large appetite, the 'plate' was also devoured. According to tradition, the Trojan hero Aeneas established the city of Lavinium on the spot where he devoured empty plates (bread plates) due to hunger.

The Vikings also ate a type of pizza, namely a round-shaped type of bread with all sorts of ingredients in it, baked in a type of pizza oven. It wasn't until the 17th century that pizza made its appearance in Naples, without the tomato sauce, of course, because at that time tomatoes were erroneously considered toxic. Tomatoes from South America were introduced in Europe around 1500 and were mostly a yellow variety. This is why the Italian name for tomato is pomo d'oro, which means 'golden apple'. The tomatoes that we see today were developed by means of cross-fertilization in the 18th century. The best-known pizza in those days was the Mastunicola, a pizza base decked with lard, pecorino, black pepper, and basil.

Most people still consider pizza Margherita the most authentic pizza. It was created by Raffaele Esposito, one of the best-known pizza makers in Naples. He had the honour of making a pizza for King Umberto I and his wife Margherita. His chauvinism inspired him to create a pizza with the colours of the Italian flag (tomato sauce, buffalo mozzarella, and basil) and that's how pizza Margherita was born.

Try this piece of Italian history at La Perla.

BREDA

Singel 210 - 1016 AB Amsterdam
T +31 20 622 5233 - www.breda-amsterdam.com
Open daily, lunch 12.00-13.00, dinner 18.00-22.00

Guillaume de Beer, Freek van Noortwijk, and Johanneke van Iwaarden were all born and raised in Breda. They work and live in Amsterdam, where they already have the gorgeous Guts&Glory, and they make Pita at their venue in the famous Foodhallen.

Tasting menu

With Breda, they want to create a relaxed, cozy atmosphere and offer a whiff of the Burgundian lifestyle of this southern city. That's why they had no problem coming up with the name of their newest restaurant. They didn't want to fill the place with artefacts and paraphernalia of the city of Breda; they aimed for the southern city's typical vibe and atmosphere. Indeed, the restaurant does not have the feel of Amsterdam. The decor is simple yet striking and looks more like a cross between a French bistro and a hip-themed restaurant in a major city.

The menu changes daily, and depending on how much time you have to spend here, you can order a basic, medium, or full-monty meal which showcases a minimum of 5 small dishes. The dishes are daring but simple, with a focus on versatile pairings, with just a few elements that excite and surprise your taste buds. Their cooking style is unique and you will see their no-waste policy throughout the menu. Creative high-level cooking under a flag of sustainability is what you can expect once you enter this gastronomical haven of peace. Don't go here if you want a quick bite; take your time, and you will be greatly rewarded.

PROEFLOKAAL A. VAN WEES

Herengracht 319 - 1016 AV Amsterdam
T + 31 20 625 4334 - www.proeflokaalvanwees.nl
Thu. 12.00-01.00, Fri.-Sat. 12.00-02.00, Wed.-Sun. 12.00-00.00

De Ooievaer was founded in 1782 and is one of the last authentic distilleries in Amsterdam's centre. Stepping inside this place is like stepping back in time.

CHEESE FONDUE

Dutch cheese fondue

Just look down at the original cobbled floor and you'll see it used to be an alley.

This tasting room was opened in 1973 by the Van Wees family as a tasting outlet for the excellent genevers made at the De Ooievaer distillery. It used to be called De Admiraal. Now it has grown into the number-one spot for discovering the very interesting and intriguing local "genever culture". A lot may have changed here, but not the way genever is made.

The Dutch played an important role in the creation of many famous liquors around the world. English Gin was created as a variant of Dutch genever, because the Dutch king of England, Willem III (650-1702), couldn't live without his fix of genever. The Dutch also founded numerous cognac distilleries in France and were the first to ship port, sherry, and madeira around the globe. They also invented the technique of distilling sugar cane, thus creating rum.

Meanwhile here at Van Wees, genever is still considered cultural heritage, so tradition is kept and cherished. You can't enjoy a taste of Amsterdam's finest without some small bites. One of the specialties here is a rich cheese fondue, made only with local cheeses. Go for the full experience.

Kef's Angels

Fromagerie

némbert · Comté · Hollande · Bresse Bleu

LAITI C°

FROMAGERIE ABRAHAM KEF

Marnixstraat 192 - 1016 TJ Amsterdam
T +31 20 420 0097 - www.abrahamkef.nl
Wed.-Thu. 11.00-19.00, Fri.-Sat. 10.00-19.00, Sun. 12.00-18.00
Tasting room Sun. 12.00-18.00, reservation mandatory

I once landed in a discussion about the quality of Italian mozzarella at Di Palo's in New York and at Orobianco in the village of Opende in the Province of Groningen.

Mozzarella di Opende
(Groningen)
'shirtless' cheese

The discussion didn't take place at a bar or a café, but at a renowned Italian restaurant famous for importing top quality Italian products. We went to Stéphane Tissot, iconic winemaker in French Jura, with the bright idea of continuing the mozzarella argument at his place. We took with us our mozzarella, carefully packaged. Since it was logistically too complicated to fly in Di Palo's product, I had brought a nice piece of Orobianco with me. With typical Italian ostentation, Tissot sliced his three top mozzarella cheeses from the Campania region and surroundings, and I did the same with the Orobianco. Plates were marked underneath, and we sampled, and sampled again, and perspired. I mean him, not me. 'This one is clearly the best,' Tissot said, 'creamy, rich milk taste, great texture, everything you expect from a mozzarella.' The cheese almost looked like a spoonful of the best ice cream, although not cold. Great was Tissot's surprise when he discovered that he had chosen the Orobianco; the other members of the improvised sampling panel were just as amazed.

Me? I was not surprised at all. The best mozzarellas I ever found were outside of Italy, namely in New York and in Opende. Orobianco people are indeed so skillful and small-scaled that mozzarella lands in your mouth only three days after the milking. Mozzarella is one of the most popular cheeses in the world. Incidentally, I wonder why there are so many types of bad mozzarella on the market. The word mozzarella comes for the Italian verb *mozzare* (which means 'to slice' or 'to cut off'). It has been made for centuries in southern Italy from the rich milk of the buffalo. It is actually the common name for two cheeses: mozzarella from buffalo milk, and fior di latte from cow milk. The term mozzarella appeared for the first time in 1570, in Bartolomeo Scappi's cookbook. However, it had already been made in 12th century convents. This cheese is sometimes called scamozzata or small scamoza, which means 'shirtless' because of the fact that it doesn't have a crust.

This terrific mozzarella can only be found in specific stores. In Amsterdam, you will find it at Erik's Delicatessen, and at Fromagerie Abraham Kef.

With their uncompromising selection of fabulous cheeses, Kef has been a must in the Amsterdam cheese world for over sixty years. The current owner, Marike van der Werff, is a passionate woman who carries on this colossal job. She only sells raw milk cheese from small producers in various countries, and she knows the story behind every cheese. Captured in a beautiful large black & white photograph, Abraham Kef looks from behind his ever present glass of red wine. And he saw that it was good.

What are you waiting for?

BALTHAZAR'S KEUKEN

Elandsgracht 108 - 1016 VA Amsterdam
T + 31 20 420 2114 - www.balthazarskeuken.nl
Tue.-Sun. 18.00-22.30

Karin Gaasterland and Alain Parry opened this opinionated restaurant in 1995. At that time, the Jordaan could really use a place like this.

Sharing plates

They turned the place into a lasting success story. The restaurant used to be a blacksmith's forge with a modern-rustic look. The decor is cosy and very inviting. The overall vibe is intimate, and it almost feels like you are eating at a friend's place.

The menu is decided for you; you only need to choose between meat and fish. The chef draws a small fish or a tiny steak knife on a kitchen tile to remember which table is having what. Karin and Alain really feel positive about what they are doing. Their dishes, interior, vibe, everything at Balthazar's Keuken tells us they have vision and passion, which is reinforced by the fact that they've never abandoned their concept.

The food is sublime and dictated by a simple philosophy: let's cook with whatever we have on hand. The creative force of the chefs has ensured a large fan base since the restaurant's beginning over 20 years ago. At Balthazar, guests are still eager to score a table, order some dishes big enough to share, and dive into them. Balthazar's Keuken is a concept statement that is here to stay.

Beulings

BEULINGS

Beulingstraat 9 - 1017 BA Amsterdam
T +31 20 320 6100 - www.beulings.nl
Wed.-Sun. 19.00-22.30

Just steps away from the '9 Straatjes' and the Bloemenmarkt is this low profile restaurant in a remote, quiet street in the bustling historic city center. The '9 straatjes' stand for nine extremely cozy and picturesque streets right in the middle of the Unesco World Heritage Canal belt.

Scallop, yakon, Jerusalem artichoke

Here, you can overview, next to unique shops and charming eateries, all building styles of the old city center, and you will be steeped back into the 17th century.

Beulings is one of those under-the-radar places that are just waiting to be discovered. Every day, the team led by Chef Bas Bont at the helm cooks a small, balanced menu, using only seasonal products. Bas Bont has learned his craftsmanship in very good Italian and French-inspired restaurants in town. La Rive, Het Tuynhuys, Segugio and Van Vlaanderen, just to name a few. He uses refined and sometimes contemporary techniques on top-notch seasonal products, which results in a fresh but artisan style of dishes. Everything here is made from scratch.

The team is on a continuous quest for deepness in their dishes, sometimes pioneering with lesser-known ingredients like this yakon. The yakon reminds me of the slightly sweet, fresh crunchiness of water chestnuts or even jicama and clearly adds an extra touch and layer of texture to the dish. This apple of the Earth or Peruvian Ground apple originates in the Andes but his adaptive qualities have made it more and more popular throughout the world.

Beulings has this halo of distinction and obvious class where you will not find four rowdy girls celebrating on a Friday night. This is the place to sit back, relax and enjoy the culinary ride. It also seems the perfect spot to take your in-laws.

LIBRIJE's ZUSJE

Waldorf Astoria - Herengracht 542-556 - 1017 CG Amsterdam
T +31 20 718 4643 - www.librijeszusje.nl
Thu.-Sat. 12.30-14.00 and 18.30-22.30

The first time I ate at De Librije was some odd 15 years ago, and two or three locations ago. I was living in Antwerp and looked on the map to find out where Zwolle was. There was no GPS back then so I estimated the distance, but was completely wrong. I was two hours early because there was no traffic at all.

Avocado sorbet

chartreuse, green apple, cucumber, yoghurt

I walked into the restaurant around 5 PM, which even at Zwolle, is not an appropriate time for dinner. I introduced myself and asked Johnnie to direct me to my hotel. I couldn't help noticing that behind my name, written in large capital letters, was the word BELG. Later, at the dinner table, Johnnie asked me what a Belgian guy from a country with great restaurants was looking for in Zwolle. That evening, I had one of the most memorable and exciting meals of my life.

Times changed quickly for Johnnie and Therese Boer. Johnnie is now considered one of the greatest chefs Holland has ever produced. When they were looking for an extension of their three-star Michelin restaurant in Amsterdam, they chose the most expensive postal code of the city, The Herengracht, right on the Golden Bend. The monumental Waldorf Astoria was more than happy to accommodate "Librije's little sister". This is Mayfair; this is the Upper East Side or the first arrondissement, this is the place to be. It was named in 1612 after the 'Heeren Regeerders van de Stad Amsterdam', the so-called governors of the city. Six of those magnificent houses form the majestic Waldorf Astoria.

To oversee their Amsterdam venue, Holland's foremost power-couple in Dutch gastronomy chose the lost son Sidney Schutte. Sidney used to be sous-chef at De Librije, before his hunger for experience pushed him towards Asia where he worked for a few years. Stronger than ever, he made his way back and is at the helm of Librije's zusje. Tasting his food, I cannot think of a reason why the place is called "Librije's little sister"! The Asian experience has made Sidney a better chef than he already was. He came back more whole, and stronger. When tasting the avocado for example, I realized this was a textural tour de force. Is it an avocado? Or is it the best avocado you ever imagined? The texture and complexity are mind-blowing.

It is of course ridiculous to choose one dish in a restaurant like this, but hey, those are the rules. Sidney masters the rare art of combining complementing textures and flavors to a higher sensorial order. On occasion, the universe will grant you a gastronomical encounter of the third kind, so mind-melting that it becomes hard to envision life without it. It turns out there's a name for this experience: the culinary art of Sidney Schutte.

Of course, Johnnie has complete faith in Sidney's abilities but when you see chefs pushing a Porsche to try to get it started in front of the Waldorf, you know that Johnnie came by for a visit. Put this restaurant on your bucket list!

PATISSERIE HOLTKAMP

Vijzelgracht 15 - 1017 HM Amsterdam
T +31 20 624 8757 - www.patisserieholtkamp.nl
Mon.-Fri. 8.30-18.00, Sat. 8.30-17.00

No, this is not an error. You are at the right address for the very best croquettes of the Netherlands. This traditional patisserie opened in 1886 at Vijzelgracht 15 and was taken over in 1969 by Cees and Petra Holtkamp.

HOLTIKAMP

CROQUETTEN VAN DE AMSTERDAMSCHE SCH

Veal croquette

a true revelation and a benchmark for all other croquettes

As a true family business (Cees at the oven and Petra in the shop), they have made a name for themselves in Amsterdam and far beyond. Also, many restaurants and grand cafés have discovered that the Holtkamp patisserie delivers much better products than they could make themselves. The current generation, Angela Holtkamp and her son-in-law Nico, are continuing the success concept. They have refreshing ideas, although they will not tamper with tradition any time soon. They often work with the other culinary wonder, Johannes van Dam. They make no secret of the fact that they owe him a lot.

The 18 square feet shop is a showpiece for art deco. In 1928, the store was decorated in this style, and in 2002 it was fully redone in its original state. I am really happy that the Holtkamps' never listened to people who tried to convince them to expand their shop. Indeed, this tiny jewel of a store is always full of people who marvel at the fabulous Sacher torte and other pies. This store is a true test for anyone who has to watch his weight. The jaw-dropping sweets from their classic, crafty repertoire include Tom pouce, lemon tart, Russian charlotte, treacle cake, chocolate vermicelli, you name it. All the classics are here.

However, we prefer to go to Holtkamp for something hearty. Since 1969, they have been making calf croquettes (spelled the old-fashioned way by Holtkamp) as part of their assortment. At the end of the eighties, they added shrimp croquettes to their repertoire, upon the request of Café Luxembourg. To achieve the perfect texture and most importantly the right flavor, they have carefully listened to the advice of distiller Cees van Wees and chef John Halvemaan.

You can buy the croquettes and bake them at home, or you can eat them at the store. Even though the shrimp croquette is unbelievably delicious in all aspects, the calf croquette is a true revelation and a benchmark for all other croquettes. The balance between the crust and the filling is perfect. The filling itself is of amazing beauty. The combination of velvety, creamy, flavorful texture and careful seasoning: this is a product where everything fits.

So, next time you are in Amsterdam, stop by Holtkamp and treat yourself to shrimp and calf croquettes to be eaten with your fingers. You will better understand what I have described. Isn't it true that a bite says more than a thousand words?

STEAKHOUSE PIET DE LEEUW

Noorderstraat 11 - 1017 TR Amsterdam
T +31 20 623 7181 - www.pietdeleeuw.nl
Mon.-Fri. 12.00-22.30, Sat.-Sun. 17.00-22.30

Since 1949, Steakhouse Piet de Leeuw has been a popular café-restaurant in Mokum with the pleasant characteristics of a pub. The atmosphere is always laid- back and pleasant.

horse tenderloin mushrooms and onions

Mokum is a popular nickname for Amsterdam. It comes from the Hebrew word *Makom* that means 'place' or 'city'. In the Dutch-Jewish language in the not-so-distant past, most cities were pronounced with the first letter in Hebrew. So, Amsterdam was Mokum Alef, meaning 'City A'. This was also the case with many other cities, although only Mokum for Amsterdam has remained in the popular language. The Jewish community definitely feels at home in Amsterdam. The many photographs of guests who loved coming here are testimony to the good times spent in this place.

Piet de Leeuw was the uncle of Loek Van Thiel, the current owner and inspiring force. Uncle Piet was a reputable horse butcher working in the centre of Amsterdam. That is why eating horse meat in its various concoctions and preparations has been a true tradition here from day one.

Owner Loek van Thiel is a passionate man, dedicated to preserving this traditional restaurant. I like to eat his horse tenderloin with mushrooms and onions.

A truly festive meal!

othing is impossible

"FISH 'N CHICKS
COWS AND PIGS

GUTS&GLORY

Utrechtsestraat 6 - 1017 VN Amsterdam
T +31 20 362 0030 - www.gutsglory.nl
Daily 18.30-22.00, closed on the first Monday of the month

Many new restaurants open with a so-called new or innovative concept. It is a pity that most of those seem to be warmed up leftovers of an already old and dry concept. This is not the case at Guts&Glory.

Free range Polderhoen

Guillaume de Beer and Freek Van Noortwijk are the creative chefs behind sister restaurant Daalder in the Jordaan. They came up with 'Fish and chicks, cows and pigs' as a concept. Their idea is as simple as it is brilliant. By focussing on a different animal every four months, they create a new and exciting restaurant every season. It is not only exciting for the patrons but also for the chefs who can focus completely on how to get the best out of the chosen ingredient.

Chapter 1 is Polderhoen, a free-range breed of chicken. This French breed, the Hubbard JA757 to be precise, was chosen because it grows very slowly with the result that the flesh is tight and full of flavour. The chickens are bred in a pure organic setting, allowing them time to grow as slowly as possible, which is better for the animal and better for the meat that will eventually end up on our plates.

This first chapter is all about this infamous chicken in all its forms and transformations. Who can resist the sight of a chicken roasted to perfection? These Rolls-Royce free-range chickens are soaked in homemade aromatic brine prior to preparation to boost the flavour. Then there's a choice between the classical approach, a whole Polderhoen roasted to perfection accompanied by sublime French Fries and a crispy fresh salad. Or you can go for the more creative approach in which every part of the chicken is featured in tasty original dishes. How about the delicious thighs, served as pulled chicken with hoisin, spicy black beans and sour cream? The Polderhoen-dog was created by Brandt & Levie and is served with sauerkraut, fried onions and homemade pickles.

For Chapter 2, Guillaume and Freek are considering fish in all its expressions. Autumn will be entirely dedicated to beef whereas winter will be all about pork.

I can hardly wait...

RIJKS

Museumstraat 2 - 1071 XX Amsterdam
T +31 20 674 7555 - www.rijksrestaurant.nl
Mon.-Sat. 11.30-15.00 and 17.00-22.00, Sun. 11.30-15.00

Adjacent to the world-famous Rijksmuseum, this stylish restaurant tries to tell the story of the Netherlands. The works hanging in the museum not only reveal the authenticity, quality, and individualism of Dutch culture, they also reflect the influence of faraway cultures.

Dry aged fillet of duck

This is the vision of Joris Bijdendijk, the handsome, charismatic and talented chef of Rijks. His dishes reproduce this very vision on the plate so that, in a way, the restaurant is an extension of the museum and the dishes are like works of art, waiting for admirers.

At the age of 16, Joris Bijdendijk had an epiphany: he was destined to be a top chef. His dream was to work in France, the Nirvana of classical cooking. But first he gained experience working with his mentor Ron Blaauw in Amsterdam. When he started working with Blaauw he told him: "I will be working for you for six years: the first three I will learn from you and you don't need to pay me, the next three you can consider me a return on your investment and I will work my ass off for you." The restaurant was awarded its first and second Michelin star with a Champions League-team.

Although still young, Bijdendijk knows what he wants and has spent half his life in the kitchen. Unlike many of his colleagues, he is very organised and feels the need to set goals, so he always knows what he is working towards. Once he achieves a goal, he sets himself a new one.

Bijdendijk had always dreamed of working at a French cooking legend, so he sold everything, bought himself a car and headed towards Paris. After 30 interviews, he became disillusioned and headed down to Lyon where, like Paris, nobody wanted to hire this Dutch guy. In Marseille, Bijdendijk's luck turned when Le Jardin des Sens, a flashy three-Michelin-starred restaurant in Montpellier, was eager to hire him. He quickly realized that working in an iconic kitchen can be like surviving out in the jungle: only the strong can do it. Bijdendijk is not a quitter, however, and he rose to the challenge of becoming a sous-chef. When Blaauw contacted him with an offer to work at The Grand Amsterdam, Bijdendijk returned to the Netherlands and, under Blaauw's guidance, ran the hotel's kitchen. In 2014, after reviving The Grand and earning it a Michelin star, Bijdendijk became executive chef at Rijks, his greatest challenge yet.

Today, Rijks is bustling and has built itself a solid reputation. It is neither fine dining nor bistronomy; it is Rijks: individual and difficult to grasp, but clearly a style and class of its own. The restaurant itself is a beautiful high-ceilinged space that operates independently from the Museum, making it easier for it to create its own identity. Bijdendijk's combinations are surprising at first, but they seem to work. Rijks is not just another restaurant in a museum; it clearly qualifies as a top-notch food destination in its own right.

居酒屋 | DE JAPAN NER

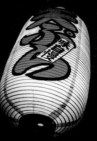

TOKYO DRIFTER

DE JAPANNER

Albert Cuypstraat 228 - 1073 BN Amsterdam
T +31 20 233 9939 - www.dejapanner.com
Sun.-Thu. 18.00-01.00, Fri.-Sat. 18.00-03.00

This place is a real hotspot.

Herring Sashimi

Not far from the statue of famous Dutch singer and folk hero André Hazes lies this bustling restaurant where Japanese izakaya-style food is served. This place proves that Japanese food doesn't have to be expensive or fancy.

The two young owners of De Japanner wanted to show that Japan has more to offer than just sushi or sashimi. They tried to create the typical atmosphere of a backstreet izakaya in one of Japan's large cities, where people meet after work for drinks and bites. Like in Japan, you can order food here till 12.30 am and at weekends till 2.30 am. Usually the place is packed with beautiful people drinking and dining at the bar or communal tables.

The kitchen staff plays with Japanese condiments as if they've done nothing else all their lives, so the food really tastes like izakaya food. The owners also created their own East Meets West. A striking example is the herring sashimi in which a classic Dutch ingredient, brined young fat herring, is pimped to a real Japanese sashimi dish, and boy, does it taste good! I'm a fan of these typical Dutch herrings and, off course, an even bigger fan of Japanese food. A combo of both is a winner.

End your meal with some urumaki, the typical inside-out rolls created by Japanese immigrants in the US. Locals don't like the look and feel of the nori on the outside of a maki. Urumaki is seldom seen in Japan, but it is a solid introduction to people who are just discovering Japanese cuisine.

A very nice, friendly, and nonchalant Japanese joint that will change your opinion of Japanese restaurants.

I amsterdam

ADDITIONAL EATERIES
CENTRE

SAMHOUD PLACES - €€€€
Oosterdokskade 5
1011 AD Amsterdam
T +31 20 260 2094
▶ www.samhoudplaces.com/nl

GEISHA - €€€€
Prins Hendrikkade 106 A
1011 AJ Amsterdam
T +31 20 626 2410
▶ www.restaurantgeisha.nl

PAPABUBBLE - €
Staalstraat 16
1011 JL Amsterdam
T +31 20 626 2662
▶ www.papabubble.nl

NEW KING - €€
Zeedijk 115-117
1012 AV Amsterdam
T +31 20 625 2180
▶ www.newking.nl

BRIDGES - €€€€
Oudezijds Voorburgwal 197
1012 EX Amsterdam
T +31 20 555 3560
▶ www.bridgesrestaurant.nl

THE WHITE ROOM - €€€€
Dam 9
1012 JS Amsterdam
T +31 20 554 9454
▶ www.restaurantthewhiteroom.com

GANDHI - €€
Damrak 54
1012 LL Amsterdam
T +31 20 638 3222
▶ www.indianrestaurantgandhi.com

PRESSROOM - €€€
Nieuwezijds Voorburgwal 67
1012 RE Amsterdam
T +31 20 627 5900
▶ www.pressroomamsterdam.com

JORDINO - €
Haarlemmerdijk 25A
1013 KA Amsterdam
T +31 20 420 3225
▶ www.jordino.nl

SHAH JAHAN - €€
Eerste Anjeliers Dwarsstraat 18
1015 NR Amsterdam
T +31 20 624 0122
▶ www.shah-jahan.nl

ENVY - €€€€
Prinsengracht 381
1016 HL Amsterdam
T +31 20 344 6407
▶ www.envy.nl

ROSIE'S - €€€
Rozengracht 214a
1016 NL Amsterdam
T +31 20 723 5144
▶ www.rosiesamsterdam.nl

PORTUGALIA - €€
Kerkstraat 35
1017 GB Amsterdam
T +31 20 625 6490
▶ www.portugalia.nl

MASHUA - €€€
Prinsengracht 703
1017 JV Amsterdam
T +31 20 420 0559
▶ www.mashua.nl

HET BUFFET VAN ODETTE - €€
Prinsengracht 598
1017 KS Amsterdam
T +31 20 423 6034
▶ www.buffet-amsterdam.nl

SUSHISAMBA AMSTERDAM - €€€€
Max Euweplein 64
1017 MB Amsterdam
T +31 20 797 1530
▶ www.sushisamba.com/location/Amsterdam

LE BOUCHON DU CENTRE - €€€
Falckstraat 3
1017 VV Amsterdam
T +31 20 330 1128
▶ www.bouchonducentreamsterdam.com

AUBERGE JEAN & MARIE - €€€
Albert Cuypstraat 58-60
1072 CV Amsterdam
T +31 20 845 2005
▶ www.aubergeamsterdam.nl

REURINGS - €€€
Lutmastraat 99
1073 GR Amsterdam
T +31 20 777 0996
▶ www.cafereuring.nl

ZAAGMOLEN - €€€
Tweede Jan Steenstraat 3HS
1073 VK Amsterdam
T +31 6 42944581
▶ www.restaurantzaagmolen.nl

VUURTORENEILAND

ZOMERRESTAURANT
Markermeer - Durgerdam
www.vuurtoreneiland.nl

May 1st-end of September, Wed.-Sat. 19.30-22.30, Sun. 12.30-15.00 & 18.30-21.30

Eating in and from nature. If you're looking for a truly exceptional dining experience, please continue reading. Every year, from May 1st, the team from restaurant As erects an elegant glass building on a truly remarkable site, only accessible by a small boat.

Eating from and with nature

Vuurtoreneiland is a very small deserted island surrounded by silence, water, light and open air. This tiny yet inspiring island is in the middle of a nature reserve, the IJdoornpolder in the Markermeer. It is remote—about 7 km from the city centre—but is still part of the municipality of Amsterdam and a unique natural feature of the city. The island is rugged, inhabited by its own microcosms of animals and rare plants. You will find here a deserted fort, a UNESCO world heritage site, and the only lighthouse in Amsterdam. Over three centuries ago, the mayor of Amsterdam commissioned the construction of the stone lighthouse on land of the Engel family who lived on the island, and in 1883 it was replaced by a cast iron lighthouse. In 1809, the small island received military status and became part of the famous Stelling van Amsterdam.

Vuurtoreneiland is not accessible to the public, but every summer the team from As builds a glass shelter where you can eat what nature provides. The local food is cooked using old artisan techniques and an open wood fire. To keep up with nature, the menu changes on a weekly basis. Cooking here is all about tradition, nature, culture, work and craftsmanship. Meat and fish are cooked and served on the bone; only local produce and high quality vegetables make it to the plate. The idea is for guests to benefit from the long-term and intense relationships this cooking team has created with its suppliers. All manipulation of the food is natural: preserving, fermenting, smoking, roasting, etc.

Eating here is more like a mini-vacation than merely going out to dinner. The island experience starts at the landmark Lloyd Hotel where you can board the historic IJveer XIII. From there, there is a five-hour long dinner experience you are not going to forget. The evenings on Vuurtoreneiland evoke a very intimate experience of which great food is an essential part. Staring at the horizon and enjoying the great wide open is also essential to this unique night out in Amsterdam.

The best five hours ever spent…

FC HYENA

Aambeeldstraat 24 - 1021 KB Amsterdam
T +31 20 363 8502 - www.fchyena.nl

Open daily from 18.00 till late night

The team behind FC Hyena keeps on surprising. They own Hotel de Goud-fazant, which is actually a restaurant; Café Modern, also a restaurant; and FC Hyena, which doesn't have a football field but two movie theatres, a wood-fired oven, and a huge wine list.

Dishes to share

In this case, FC stands for Film Club. The founders of FC Hyena, Lotte Smit and her husband Joris Brieffies, always dreamed of having a film club that would also serve as a restaurant and where guests could enjoy wine while watching their favourite films. In case you were wondering why they called it Hyena, it was because they liked the font in a postal-stamp set that they had, but many of the letters were missing. Fhinac and Financyen were two options, but they ultimately decided on Hyena.

Inspired by the cinema-with-restaurant concept of the Electric Cinema on Portobello Road in London, FC Hyena boasts two movie theatres, one with 60 seats and another with 105 seats.

The theatres have a full bar where you can also order light bites of delicious tacos, grilled oysters, and more, all prepared by a Mexican chef in a wood-fired oven. To complement your food you can order a natural wine from the remarkable wine list. The movie theatres have a twist: there are no chairs but custom-made benches that seat 15 each. How cool is that!

It goes without saying that the bar in the larger theatre closes during the actual film. With regards to the food, I think the fact that there's an actual Thai soccer team called FC Hyena is pure coincidence. This is one of those places that keeps you up at night regretting you didn't come up with its brilliant concept yourself.

HANGAR

Ambeeldstraat 36 - 1021 KB Amsterdam
T + 31 20 363 8657 - www.hangar.amsterdam
Sun.-Thu. 10.00-01.00, Fri.-Sat. 10.00-03.00

How to turn an abandoned parking lot into a crowd-pleasing restaurant?
Tim Immers and Jop Pollmann pulled it off in seven weeks.

Eggs Benedict

When the green corrugated iron for building the hangar was delivered, both men where a little disappointed; they wanted more of a raw look that would blend in with the rough-and-raw Noord neigbourhood. So they drove the delivery truck to a nearby farm and made a strange deal with the farmer. They traded their corrugated iron sheets for the farmer's used rusty ones, giving the place a unique identity. Still, the main attraction is the chef: they managed to seduce Ricardo van Ede into becoming their executive chef.

Ricardo is one of the bad boys of Dutch gastronomy. He is in every way a remarkable man. His reputation precedes him and he's known as the chef who was awarded a Michelin star at the age of 21. This is an extraordinary achievement, yet it would be more than unfair to limit Ricardo's immense talent and career to this one accomplishment.

Many acclaimed gastronomical critics classify Ricardo's food under the New Raw movement. In my opinion, his food impersonates this movement. I have profound admiration for chefs who are able to express themselves through food and stretch their creativity to the limit. But I also admire Ricardo for the artisan quality of his extremely countrified dishes that actually have a refreshing lack of creativity. This bohemién is teaching us to taste again and to give guests what they really want: a plate of real food that makes you emotional and nostalgic at the same time.

Ricardo is without any doubt one of the best chefs of this generation and all the food he touches turns into something magical.

HOTEL DE GOUDFAZANT

Aambeeldstraat 10 H - 1021 KB Amsterdam
T +31 20 636 5170 - www.hoteldegoudfazant.nl
Tue.-Sun. from 18.00. Closed on Mondays.

When you hear the name of this place, you imagine an old school, kitsch and over-the-top hotel. You would never expect this swanky, industrial-chic space where the open kitchen serves creative dishes balancing between French and what I would call contemporary Dutch cuisine.
A Porsche 911 and a Citroen DS nonchalantly parked outside the restaurant remind us that this space used to be a car shop.

Black Angus Hanger steak,
asparagus, gratin dauphinois, horse mushrooms, port sauce

Niels Wouters, the founder of Hotel de Goudfazant pioneered in bringing trendy gastronomy to the Amsterdam-North district. Hotel de Goudfazant's vibe is raw, industrial, sexy, and trendy. The interior is gutted and boasts exposed rusty beams that seem to be very comfortably seated beside a glass chandelier made out of old milk bottles.

The view from this part of the water is overwhelming, especially when there's a lot of traffic between the restaurant and Kompaseiland. The refurbished warehouse is a gastronomical oasis in disguise between unsightly industrial buildings on the IJ waterfront. When this place opened back in 1996, even Niels' closest friends thought he'd gone mad, opening such an important venue on this side of the city. Nevertheless, ten years later it seems perfectly normal for locals to catch the ferry over here just to eat.

Why is there a picture of Jacques Brel in the restaurant? This multi-million record selling Belgian singer-songwriter gained tremendous status throughout the world with his sensitive, literate, intelligent, theatrical songs. He is considered the master of modern French chanson and, although he only recorded in French and Dutch, he influenced people like David Bowie, Leonard Cohen, Ray Charles, Nina Simone, Frank Sinatra, and many more. Brel is one of those artists who are very hard to cover or translate. Poetry is exactly that part which gets lost in translation. When you look outside, you spot the first Brel reference, cause you're *in the Port of Amsterdam, There's a sailor who sings, Of the dreams that he brings, From the wide open sea, In the port of Amsterdam, There's a sailor who sleeps, While the river bank weeps, To the old willow tree.* Thanks to David Bowie who provided this translation. The name of the restaurant itself is part of one his iconic songs: *Les Bourgeois.* This song was written in 1962 and tells the story of young men who spend their evenings drinking in a pub before drunkenly mooning at and verbally abusing a few lawyers they see leaving the bar of a hotel across the street. That hotel, where they end up drinking and getting yelled at themselves in a further stage of their lives, was the Hotel de Goudfazant. The translation goes something like this: *Then when midnight chimed, lawyers we could mock, Stepped out of the Hotel de Goudfazant, We dropped our trousers down and we kindly bowed, Singing this song, Upper class, you can kiss my arse, As you older grow, even less you know, Upper class, you can kiss my arse... Just like pigs you grunt, you're a load of...*

It may seem odd, but you cannot book a room here. The food served has a more intimate feel to it. 'Never compromise on quality' seems to be the motto in this trendsetting restaurant that clearly is off the beaten track in every meaning of the word.

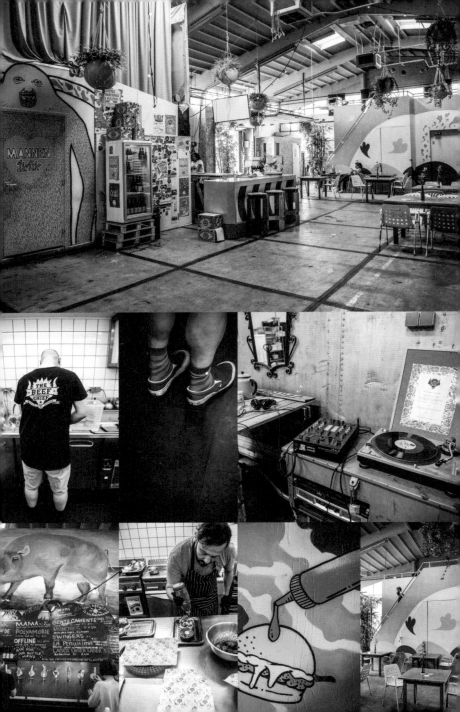

THE BEEF CHIEF
(INSIDE OEDIPUS BREWERY)

Gedempt Hamerkanaal 85 A - 1021 KP Amsterdam
T +31 6 199 97846 - www.thebeefchief.com

Thu.-Sat. 17.00-21.00, Sun. 16.00-20.00

Amsterdam's best burgers are served from a 1975 Citroen H van. It doesn't take much to make an award-winning burger, only excellent beef, homemade kimchi, and a lot of passion. Simon Parrott was born and raised in England, but he fell in love with street food in Berlin. Love brought him to Holland.

Kimchi Burger

This hippie (or anti-hippie) van is producing one of the best burgers in the country, and it is surely the best hamburger joint without a brick-and-mortar address. All ingredients are locally sourced and all excel in quality. The Beef Chief's kimchi is, of course, also homemade. Kimchi is probably one of the oldest dishes known to man. Its origin dates back to the early Three Kingdoms period. A Chinese text published in 289 AD refers to the Goguryeo people (the Koreans) as being very skilled in making fermented foods such as wine, miso-salted fish, and vegetables fermented in a pickle jar. This indicates that fermented vegetables were widely eaten in that period. A poem about Korean pickled radishes written by Yi Gyubo in the 13th century reveals that radish kimchi was very common in Goryeo.

One of the most moving moments I have ever witnessed on TV is a scene in which a shabbily dressed father, having saved money for an entire year, drives a dilapidated bus for three days to buy each of his children a cheeseburger at the newly opened McDonald's in Harare. What magic...

Most people think that Ronald McDonald invented the hamburger, but that is far from the truth. Ghengis Khan and his grandson Kublai travelled with pieces of beef under their horse saddles during their conquests. The constant rubbing made the meat very tender, turning it into ground meat. When Kublai Khan arrived in Moscow, he mixed egg and onion into the meat and the first burger was born.

But who was the official inventor of the hamburger? Perhaps it was Otto Kuase, a caterer from Hamburg who, in 1891, made a round roll with fried minced beef, onions, a sauce, and an egg sunny side up. German seamen introduced this goody to the US. Or maybe it was Delmonico's, a NYC steakhouse that for the first time put hamburger on its menu in 1826. Or it may have been Frank and Charles Menches, who in 1885 at the Erie County Fair in Hamburg, NY, shaped sausage meat into round forms and placed it between two slices of bread. There is evidence to believe that the first hamburger sold in a bun can be attributed to Oscar Weber Bilby from Tulsa, Oklahoma, who sold fried meat balls between bread slices during the 1891 Fourth of July festivities. The nameplate of Tulsa, Oklahoma, reads: The Real Birthplace of the Hamburger!

Seymour, Wisconsin, became home to a large group of German immigrants, and one of them, Charlie Nagreen, aka Hamburger Charlie, sold hamburgers in a roll to passersby at fairs and conventions.

In 1940, a company that would forever change the world's concept of food came up with a great idea: Richard (Dick) and Maurice (Mac) McDonald opened their first restaurant in San Bernardino, California, on the corner of 14th and E Streets. 18 years later, they had sold 100 million hamburgers.

Give me the Beef Chief's version anytime!

ercedes: Get grill regulator & fit. ♡

HEY AMIGO,
I WAS here
1916 you waren't ...
one LOVE,
Vic.

- B
- DI
- N
- LO

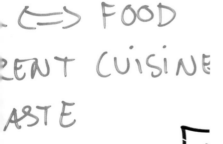

ADDITIONAL EATERIES
NORTH

RESTAURANT COBA TAQUERIA - €€
Schaafstraat 4
1021 KE Amsterdam
T +31 6 45782010
▸ www.facebook.com/Coba

STORK - €€€€
Gedempt Hamerkanaal 201
1021 KP Amsterdam
T +31 20 634 4000
▸ www.restaurantstork.nl

CAFÉ MODERN - €€€
Meidoornweg 2
1031 GG Amsterdam
T +31 20 494 0684
▸ www.modernamsterdam.nl

PENSION HOMELAND

Gebouw 006, Kattenburgerstraat 5 - 1018 Amsterdam
T + 31 20 723 2550 - www.pensionhomeland.com
Open daily, breakfast 07.00-12.00, lunch 12.00-15.30, dinner 18.00-22.30

This is a real haven right in the centre of the city. Next to the beautiful Scheepvaartmuseum lies the old Navy yard that started building warships to protect the VOC commercial fleet in 1655.

Daily changing three course menu

In fact, the Scheepvaartmuseum is the former warehouse where all the parts were stored. In those days, Amsterdam was one of the biggest and most important ports in the world. Shipbuilding stopped in 1915 and the place was turned into an officers' home. Building number 006 has been thoroughly remodeled and now boasts a gorgeous café-room hotel and an on-premises brewery.

Old satellite pictures show it as a blurred spot on the Oosterdok, but now it is accessible to everybody. A huge gate welcomes all, and just a few steps away from the extremely busy Kattenburgerstraat waits a fountain with trees and grass, secluded from the city.

The entire place is decorated in fifties and sixties style. A true vintage palace with a flair for detail when it comes to decor. The decorators really went the extra mile, even adding the typical ficus tree, a tropical plant popular in the Netherlands in the sixties. The entire place evokes your grandparents' home. It also makes me regret that I threw out all my old stuff. This could have been the interior of my home. But if you think they kept the interior as it was, think again. Every item in the restaurant was purchased from antique stores and websites selling second-hand items. The restaurant welcomes you at the burning fireplace with an impressive range of large candles. The food is classic and you can enjoy breakfast, lunch, and dinner there. There's a daily changing fixed-price menu inspired by a combination of Mediterranean and local influences. All menu and à la carte dishes are home-made by chefs who are really passionate about their work.

The small brewery revives a centuries-old tradition. In the VOC days, ships carried golden beer over the ocean in barrels. Now the microbrewery makes small batches of artisan beer in beautiful, handcrafted bottles.

Go for the whole experience.

MAMA MAKAN
(AT THE HYATT REGENCY)

Spinozastraat 61 - 1018 HJ Amsterdam
T +31 20 554 1250 - www.mamamakan.com
Mon.-Fri. 06.30-22.30, Sat.-Sun. 07.00-22.30

At Mama Makan it's all about fine dining with Indonesian influence and inspiration. Step inside this haven of peace in Amsterdam's Spinoza Hotel, let it take you on a journey to times gone by, and experience the joys of European and Indonesian fare.

Mama's rice table

Mama Makan evokes the atmosphere of a Dutch Grand Café in Indonesia, with its striking mix of aromas and tastes. The authentic menu is reminiscent of the menus on the walls of cafés in Jakarta.

Indonesian cuisine has been downgraded to food that people take out when they don't want to cook, and it has often become a tasteless heap of unidentifiable food. However, there are many restaurateurs who want to preserve traditional Indonesian cuisine, and one of them is executive chef Paul Verheul, who honours Indonesian food by delivering beautiful dishes full of authentic flavours. In charge of this is a very authentic dynamic lady who used to run the kitchen at the Hyatt in Jakarta. She delivers great authentic food

The restaurant itself is beautiful and aims to add culinary sparkle to the neighbourhood.

The interior is simply gorgeous, with a lot of green, a phenomenal open kitchen, a chef's table, and large round tables with the typical Lazy Susan turntable in the middle of the table so that all the food is within reach. This contemporary grand café ultimately connects its customers with the local heritage, community, and history of the neighbourhood. The interior's theme enables diners to imagine the journeys on the ancient trading routes. The space makes you feel right at home. The refined furniture collection supports the restaurant's theme.

Mama Makan is unlike most hotel restaurants. Go and discover this Amsterdam East gem.

MEDIAMATIC ETEN

Dijksgracht 6 - 1019 BS Amsterdam
T +31 20 638 9901 - www.mediamatic.net
Mon.-Thu. 16.00-21.30 (only menu), Wed.-Fri. 16.00-21.30 (only pizza),
Sat. 16.00-21.30 (only menu), Sun. 16.00-21.30 (only pizza)

Moments before your train rolls into Amsterdam's Central Station, coming
in from the east, you can't help noticing huge greenhouses right next to
Hannekes Boom.

Vegan inspired dishes

This is the Mediamatic complex, where a sustainable food-production system combines the farming of vegetables and fish. Everything grown in the Aquaponics greenhouse is destined for the restaurant, which only uses ingredients produced ecologically and sustainably.

The greenhouse is a closed ecosystem with its own biosphere. The water from the fish tanks is pumped through the plant beds as irrigation. The fish poo fertilizes the plants and these, in turn, purify the water. It is a very intelligent urban system because it uses a minimal amount of space and very limited amounts of water. Mediamatic is exemplary

and is doing innovative work on sustainability and biotechnology. The same building houses a research centre for olfactory art, research and design, a secretopia, a brewery, and a fermentation centre.

The catch of the day is always local and is caught by the last remaining fisherman still fishing in the IJ, Piet Ruijter. The food is cooked in a specially designed stove called the Rocket. The restaurant is a light, bright space with a spectacular view. The menu is vegan friendly and great pizzas come out of the clay oven. The vibe in this place is unique. Although it looks very simple, it creates an atmosphere that attract diners.

RIJSEL

Marcusstraat 52B - 1091 TK Amsterdam
T +31 20 463 2142 - www.rijsel.com
Tue.-Sat. from 18.00

A rotisserie is a great kitchen appliance that fortunately is back in vogue. Who doesn't feel hungry when seeing a bunch of chicken becoming crispier at each turn of the rotisserie? You will not find a simpler and tastier food.

perfect flavor and tasteful presentation

Spring chick on the spit or poussin à la broche

Just the thought of crispy chicken skin, followed by a bite into a juicy chicken thigh is enough to give you goose bumps, or shall we say chicken bumps.

At Rijsel, the rotisserie is central in the kitchen and no matter what is in it, it is always the headliner on the kitchen stage. Here, the boss is Chef Iwan Driessen. He uses a very simple formula for success that many restaurants still overlook: serving flavor and real food to the guests. His kitchen is not based on junk food, but on stock as it was in the golden days of great French cuisine. When you have one of these stocks, a very good main ingredient and one or two accents, you can go very far in creating a dish for which people will be happy to walk the distance.

In this classic seventies interior in an old school building, they serve affordable, no-nonsense food, and that is exactly what I'm looking for in a restaurant. The relaxed yet professional atmosphere is a true crowd-pleaser and everyone eats with pleasure. Host Pieter Smits does the rest.

This low-profile restaurant keeps impressing me with its choice of dishes, perfect flavors and tasteful presentation.

No baloney here, only authenticity.

ANTEP SOFRASI

Borneostraat 92A - 1094 CP Amsterdam
T +31 20 337 8499 - www.gaziantepsofrasi.nl
Tue.-Thu. 16.00-01.00, Fri.-Sat. 16.00-03.00, Sun. 16.00-01.00

There are not many Turkish restaurants where the renowned Turkish cuisine gets the honor it deserves. The diversity characterizing Turkish gastronomy is directly linked to the numerous invasions by foreign peoples who each brought their own cooking style.

Cartlak ———————→ the power of simplicity

Moreover, the Oghuz tribes from Central Asia, together with the expanding Ottoman and Seljuq empires, integrated a great number of population groups, simultaneously adopting their culinary specialties.

Proof of this is the gigantic kitchen in the Topkapi Palace, one of Istanbul's biggest crowd-pullers. In this kitchen, all sorts of 'exotic' delights were prepared for the sultans and their entourage, while in the poor Turkish countryside local customs and cooking methods were preserved.

When you stroll through the great urban park in Gaziantep – one of the largest parks in the world – you can feel the rich history of the fifth largest city of Turkey. Many older people still name the city Antep. The prefix 'Gazi' was added in 1920 after the Turkish War of Independence. Gazi actually means warrior, and 'Antep' comes from the Arabic Ayintab, which means 'good source'. Combined, the word means 'everlasting source'.

And that it is! An everlasting source of inspiration resulting from cultural diversity: the Hittite Empire, the Greek Empire, the Persian Empire, the Byzantine Empire, and of course, the Ottoman Empire. All these high-minded cultures combined produced a local cuisine that is a true adventure, and this is what makes this restaurant so unique.

Istanbul is one of my favorite foodie destinations. I absolutely love it. But one thing is certain: I will never again eat Turkish food or kebab in Belgium or the Netherlands. I have been disappointed so many times with the insipid imitations of the real thing that are served in the Low Countries that I am totally done with it. There are a few exceptions: I think of Has Pide in Brussels, and Abooov in Ghent. But in my experience, the best Turkish meals are generally found in people's homes. But when I entered Antep Sofrasi for the first time, my kebab appetite quickly came back. The stews, all the grilled dishes, and then, of course, the kebabs will give you a true WOW feeling.

The origin of the kebab is not entirely clear. Every country in the Middle East seems to take credit for its invention. I think the Persian soldiers of a few centuries before Christ are the most credible inventors. Of course, we know that the döner kebab we see today, with the vertical spit, was created in Bursa in 1870 by Mr. Iskender. He invented the slow-rotating spit planted over a powerful fire. Indeed, the word döner means to spin.

A very unique dish at Antep Sofrasi is cartlak. We are talking about lamb liver, kidney and heart, chopped and perfectly seasoned. This dish is a beautiful illustration of the power of simplicity. Add a few raw vegetables and a piece of lavas (Turkish bread) and you have a feast of a meal. Or rather part of a feast, because at Antep Sofrasi you will give in to many more temptations. Guaranteed.

MERKELBACH

Middenweg 72 - 1097 BS Amsterdam
T +31 20 423 3930 - www.restaurantmerkelbach.nl
Tue.-Sat. 8.30-23.00, Sun.-Mon. 8.30-18.00

In the wonderful park that also hosts the De Kas restaurant, you can find the last remaining country estate within city limits: Huize Frankendael. It was built in the 17th century and is surrounded by a romantic park which has two historic gardens, a period garden and a landscape garden.

Ballotine of Chaamse hoen with ramsons

The impressive Huize Frankendael is in the middle of the park and the restaurant is located in the right wing coach house. Although the rapid and dramatic urbanization of Amsterdam now has the park completely surrounded, you can still enjoy the sound of silence and the combination of nature, gastronomy, and culture.

The restaurant is named after former city architect Ben Merkelbach. However, the first impression of the restaurant may be quite different to what you actually get. You will find here a very passionate and talented chef, Geert Burema, who is a true purist. He embraces Slow Food in its purest form, and he co-founded the Slow Food Chefs Alliance in The Netherlands. Great food is in no way elitist. The restaurant has to be a place of social lubrication, where knowledge can be spread like the gospel. Diners can appreciate where the food is actually coming from. Delicious, pure, and honest dishes from sustainable seasonal and local quality products are his mantras. Geert is a brilliant authentic chef with great vision throughout his dishes. He's a 'nose to tail' aficionado and the 'Goede Vissers' from Lauwersoog provide him with great fish from their daily catch.

One of his major projects is intense collaboration with a small farm in order to breathe new life into the Chaamse hoen, a nearly extinct chicken breed. The idea is as simple as it is brilliant. By putting the Chaamse hoen back on the menu, you create a demand, hence saving it from extinction. How it was developed is not very clear, although we are quite sure it originated from Campine (De Kempen) fowls. Throughout the centuries these Campine breeds with their specific characteristics spread from the coastal areas far into the Ardennes, mainly through monasteries located throughout the country.

In those days, it was quite common to name each breed after its area of origin. References to area-specific Campine breeds like the Hoogstraatse hoen and the Kempische hoen may be found in a number of old books, along with the Chaamse hoen, Chapons from Breda (read: Chaamse hoen). The Bertram Company from Breda raised and slaughtered birds known to be Chaamse hoen, because of the fineness of their meat and the superior flavor. The Chaamse hoen was so popular, it was often on the menu of the Royal family, and in 1881 King William III ordered a large flock of Chaamse hoen from the Bertram Company. The Chaamse hoen was standardized around 1909-1911 and in 1911 the breed was accepted into the Dutch Poultry Standards. And now this once so popular race needs help and Geert is cooking phenomenal dishes with it.

ADDITIONAL EATERIES
EAST

SCHEEPSKAMEEL - €€€
Kattenburgerstraat 7
1018 JA Amsterdam
T +31 20 337 9680
▶ www.scheepskameel.nl

THE BRUNCHROOM - €€
Czaar Peterstraat 74
1018 PR Amsterdam
T +31 20 737 1691
▶ www.facebook.com/brunchroom

WILDE ZWIJNEN - €€€€
Javaplein 23
1095 CJ Amsterdam
T +31 20 463 3043
▶ www.wildezwijnen.com

JACOBSZ - €€
Ringdijk 1A
1097 AA Amsterdam
T +31 6 42 454 677
▶ www.jacobsz.amsterdam

LA VALLADE - €€€
Ringdijk 23
1097 AB Amsterdam
T +31 20 665 2025
▶ www.lavallade.nl

DE KAS - €€€
Kamerlingh Onneslaan 3
1097 DE Amsterdam
T +31 20 462 4562
▶ www.restaurantdekas.nl

DE LOBBY FIZEAUSTRAAT - €€€
Fizeaustraat 2
1097 SC Amsterdam
T +31 20 758 5275
▶ www.thelobbyfizeaustraat.nl

TAIKO

NTEMPORARY ASIAN CUISINE
BY SCHILO

TAIKO
@ CONSERVATORIUM HOTEL

Van Baerlestraat 27 - 1071 AN Amsterdam
T +31 20 570 0000 - www.conservatoriumhotel.com/taiko-restaurant
Mon.-Sat. 18.30-22.30

I first came across a taiko drum while working in Kyoto. I was completely blown away by the performance of Kodo, arguably the best percussion group walking the face of the earth. I had never seen such combination of rhythm, control and sense of harmony.

Contemporary Asian

Schilo style

The members of the Sado Island based Kodo are all masters of the Taiko drum. Taiko are part of Japanese and Korean folklore and mythology. Historical records suggest that taiko was introduced to Japan through Korean and Chinese cultural exchange programs in the 6th century. They are also very similar to some percussion instruments seen in India. The taiko in ancient Japan were used as a means of communication and for religious and ceremonial purposes.

Schilo Van Coevorden is a remarkable chef. This Amsterdam-born scintillatingly creative chef continues to surprise both friends and foe. Severely influenced by the time he spent in Asia, this globetrotter arrived at the Conservatorium Hotel to provide us with one of the best Asian restaurants in the city and beyond. Taiko is a sleek and sexy Asian restaurant inside the glorious hotel. The design of the restaurant is stunningly beautiful. But the most spectacular achievement of this Japanese oasis is clearly its top-quality kitchen. It puzzles me how Van Coevorden manages to infuse the complex Japanese cuisine philosophy into all of his dishes. I am constantly amazed at how the kitchen manages to create such a plethora of complex Japanese and other South-Asian preparations for such a large number of enthusiastic diners. Here the plates are dressed up with frightful precision.

The kitchen develops its own style —thanks to the perceptive diligence of Schilo. Although the dishes are still very much Japanese, the kitchen tries to incorporate subtle touches from other Asian gastronomic vernaculars. Try the Forbidden soup, and you will fully understand my admiration for this man. Japanese dishes are reviewed and restyled, but what is ultimately served comes straight from the mind and heart of a chef who clearly knows what he wants.

One of the things that you want to do before you shuffle off this mortal coil is to eat here. The best Asian food made by a non-Asian chef.

CAFÉ CARON

Frans Halsstraat 28 - 1072 BS Amsterdam
T +31 20 675 8668 - www.cafecaron.nl

Open daily 18.00-01.00

A piece of France in the heart of Amsterdam. This is a real family restaurant in the sense that the entire Caron family works here, in the finest French countryside tradition.

Coquelet Café Caron

The Carons are real Frenchies and their place reflects this. The restaurant has a laid-back, relaxed ambience, and excellent, abundant food and wine. No fancy French cuisine but down-to-earth French bistro-style cooking we all adore.

Café Caron offers diners a moment of frenchification and classic French cooking by a native who knows the drill. Here, you will not be served arty-farty towers of food, but a plateful of food expressing terroir and taste. Café Caron is the perfect place to gently let the evening pass by while celebrating life with friends. The Carons strongly believe that food is the best social lubricant possible. Eating and drinking (there is an extensive wine list with some hidden gems in a small handwritten booklet) brings people together and creates lifelong friendships.

The menu follows the seasons and boasts the best of France, a collection of the things we travel to France to experience. Café Caron together with the De Pasteibakkerij are the two most French places in Amsterdam, reflecting both the food and philosophy of a great nation of bon vivants who settle their arguments over a good glass of wine.

C'est bon, c'est Caron!

· IZAKAYA · ASIAN KITCHEN & BAR ·

SIR Albert®

LIKE ALL GREAT TRAVELLERS I HAVE SEEN MORE THAN I REMEMBER AND REMEMBER MORE THAN I HAVE SEEN

BENJAMIN DISRAELI

IZAKAYA

Albert Cuypstraat 2-6 - 1072 CT Amsterdam
T +31 20 305 3090 - www.izakaya-amsterdam.com
Lunch Mon.-Fri. 12.00-14.30, Sat. 12.00-15.00, Sun. 12.00-16.00
Dinner Sun.-Wed. 18.00-23.00, Thu.-Sat. 18.00-23.30

The word 'izakaya' has been more commonly used in English and Dutch since 1987. The origin of the word is Japanese and is composed of 'i', that means 'stay', and 'sakaya', which actually is a sake shop or sake brewery.

Unagi kabayaki with foie gras and apple balsamic vinegar

In the past, some sake shopkeepers allowed their customers to sit down and drink sake, but to prevent them getting drunk too quickly, they began serving it with appetizers. In Japan, these places were usually called 'akachōchin' (which means red lantern) because most of them had a red lantern by the front door.

In the trendy De Pijp district, there is no red lantern by the front door. Here, the traditional Japanese izakaya is somewhat reinvented. Inspired by the five traditional Japanese elements—earth, water, fire, wind, and emptiness—this place offers a stylish and energetic interior. The owner of Izakaya, well-known international businessman Yossi Eliyahoo, left no detail to chance in giving his restaurant an innovative character. Hiring top chef Hariprasad Shetty was a smart move. This highly talented and sensitive chef won his spurs at Nobu in London. He is a true walking encyclopedia in the field of Japanese ingredients and dishes. Nobu inspired him to combine Japanese elements to perfection.

In Japan, an izakaya is one of the cornerstones of Japanese social culture. Izakaya in De Pijp is on the same path: this restaurant has become a reference for varied and innovative Japanese food in Amsterdam. The repertoire designed by top chef Hari is very diverse and impressive. His sakana or otsumame is simply sublime. In traditional Japan, these appetizers are specifically prepared to be served with sake. Sushi and sashimi are good, and careful attention has been given to dishes prepared in the robata grill. The idea here is not only to grill a piece of meat or fish on the specially built grill, but also to use the softly smoldering binchotan charcoal as added flavoring. During the Genroku period (1688-1704), this high-grade charcoal was manufactured for the first time by Bitchū-ya Chōzaemon in Tanabe, in the Wakayama Prefecture. He only uses very old ubame oak trees. With this high quality charcoal, popular with robata, yakitori, and unagi chefs, the pieces of charcoal can steam at very high temperatures. The typical small Japanese hotplate, or hibachi, is also reinstated in this restaurant. My favorite dish is Hari's preparation of caramelized eel combined with foie gras and apple balsamic vinegar. I firmly believe that every gastronomic institution has its own specialty and I have never found, anywhere in the world, a better eel recipe than the Japanese unagi kabayaki: a delicious preparation in which the eel is not skinned, but filleted. The filet is then grilled in one piece, steamed, and caramelized to heavenly delight. The recipe was found in the eighth century *Man'yōshū*, the oldest anthology of Japanese poems. This eel, with its very unique flavor, is combined with buttery foie gras and a drizzle of sour apple balsamic vinegar to ensure the perfect balance of the dish. At Izakaya, they create an impressive version of the best eel recipe in the world.

If you want breakfast in bed sleep in the kitchen.

We've done the resear

The egg was first

OMELEGG

Ferdinand Bolstraat 143 - 1072 LH Amsterdam
T +31 20 370 1134 - www.omelegg.com
Mon.-Fri. 07.00-16.00, Sat.-Sun. 08.00-16.00

The very first omelette restaurant in Amsterdam claims to have done
the research: the egg came first.

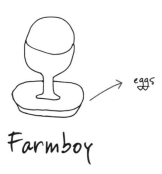

eggs

Farmboy

Eggs? We take them so much for granted that we've actually stopped thinking about how versatile and delicious they are, whether boiled, scrambled, fried, or smoked. This restaurant puts the egg on a pedestal and adds a new ingredient to the growing list of mono-dish restaurants.

We tend to associate eggs with breakfast, so you could consider Omelegg an all-day breakfast joint. I, however, see eggs from a much broader perspective than merely as breakfast food, and I enjoy them cooked in different ways. The menu at Omelegg really reflects this.

Nima and Faraz Ghorbani came up with the idea of creating an all-omelette restaurant in Amsterdam during a boring drive to Poland. More than 3,000 eggs a week are broken in this restaurant, finding their way into one of the 22 different omelettes on the menu. Yet it's not as simple as it seems. For many chefs, the challenge in making a perfect omelette is producing the right texture. Nima and Faraz wanted to take it one step further and create a farm in the city, hence the wood and reed used in the décor, evoking outdoor country life.

Egg in Brooklyn and Eggslut in L.A. are testimony to the many possibilities for egg restaurants, and this venue in trendy De Pijp is no less so.

YAMAZATO

Ferdinand Bolstraat 333 - 1072 LH Amsterdam
T +31 20 678 7450 - www.okura.nl/okura-culinair/yamazato
lunch Mon.-Sun. 12.00-14.00, dinner Mon.-Sun. 18.00-21.30

Hotel Okura is a renowned Japanese bastion that almost equals the legendary service of the 'land of the rising sun'. His high-class hotel wouldn't exist without a few top-class restaurants. On the top floor there is a culinary temple, the Ciel Bleu restaurant. However, the true jewel, the Yamazato restaurant, is on the ground floor and it is the best Japanese restaurant in Europe.

Kaiseki

Yamazato means 'small mountain village' and, strangely enough, some of the dishes as well as the calm that reigns here make me think of some mountain villages in hilly, woody parts of Japan.

Chef Oshima has been a staple in and out of the country since 1971; however, he passed the baton a few years ago to the very talented and driven Masanori Tomikawa. To enter this gastronomic seventh heaven you need the magic code: 'kaiseki'. Kaiseki is the highest form of Japanese gastronomic art and one of the most spectacular foods you can ever have on your plate.

The first literary mention of kaiseki is found in the *Man'Yoshu,* an anthology of poems from the 7th century. At the center of the 'honzen', or main table, stood a large bowl of rice around which seven side dishes were arranged. It was surrounded by seven smaller tables per person, covered with small dishes. That's a total of 35 dishes per person, reserved and eaten according to the strictest etiquette of the court of Kyoto. This was called 'honzen ryori'.

A logical evolution of this tradition is the 'cha-kaiseki ryori' that emerged during the rise of the tea ceremonies in the early 16th century. During the ceremony, attendants eat small, simple, mostly vegetarian snacks to accompany green tea. Kaiseki is a compound word: 'kai' means 'pocket' and 'seki' means 'stone'. This refers to zen monks who carried a warm stone in the pockets of their garments to fight their hunger pangs.

In sharp contrast with the 'honzen', the food served at tea ceremonies is extremely simple. It reflects nature and seasons, where human feelings are expressed in a subtle way. Water plays a central role. First, kumidashi is served (with herb or flower flavored warm water). Water is again served in (miso) soup, sake, hashidarai (water to clean your chopsticks), tea and finally water with cooked rice and salt. To get the ideal kaiseki feeling, look outside and see what nature looks and feels like, and see its reflection on your plate: colors, atmosphere and fragrance. The whole plate is an experience that arouses your senses.

A beautiful reflection of personal expression is the azukebachi (literally meaning 'entrusted') where the chef leaves the room while attendants philosophize over the dish. From the 17th century on, we find the expression 'kaiseki ryori' in Edo (Tokyo's old name), where restaurants began to expand at the beginning of the 17th century and created the golden mean between the decadent honzen and the sober, minimalist food served at tea ceremonies. Etiquette was no longer as strict. This style quickly became popular among all classes of the population. Rice and soup were served at the end.

LE HOLLANDAIS

Amsteldijk 41 - 1074 HV Amsterdam
T +31 20 679 1248 - www.lehollandais.nl
Tue.-Sat. 18.00-22.30

Le Hollandais is situated on the Amstel River, on the outskirts of the Amsterdam Quartier Latin, De Pijp. It is a very discrete restaurant where food speaks for itself. The vibe in this pleasant place is informal and spontaneous.

JAZZ*

Rabbit with black pudding

You will not easily find tourists in this 'foodtopia' because it is one of those marvelous places only local gourmets find their way too.

Chef de cuisine Adriaan van Raab van Canstein has two passions: Jazz and cooking. His restaurant features a Hammond organ right by the entrance where Adriaan tends to play a little at the end of an evening. He is proud of having great Jazzmen like Joey de Francesco and Lonny Smith amongst his regular diners. He goes completely berserk when they decide to give a spontaneous guest performance.

Who remembers Albert Spica? He was the gangster who took over the high class restaurant Le Hollandais, run by French chef Richard Boarst. We are of course in the Greenaway classic *The Cook, The Thief, His wife & Her Lover.*

When Adriaan opened Le Hollandais in 1996, he used Greenaway as an inspiration for its name. He perfected his French classic cuisine repertoire at Bordewijk, where the brilliant Wil Demandt taught him the finesse of essential French cooking. The Hollandais signature style is classic provincial French cooking with a preference for transforming offal into sexy dishes. He spent two years in charge of a small village restaurant in Southwest France where he learned to appreciate working with local and seasonal produce. This experience and Wil are the unmistakable influences in his cooking language today. He made a trade mark out of his homemade sausages, which are often served as a first course. They tend to have classic but surprising combinations like squid and pork or boudin blanc with rabbit. They stem from the same rich tradition as cassoulet, chou farci and crépinettes (packages of raw oysters and minced pork). Traditions get passed on. Adriaan used to have two people working in his kitchen, Geert Van Wersch and Jiri Brandt. Those two youngsters got more and more excited about making their own salamis and sausages. They later decided to create Brandt & Levie.

When in Rome do as the Romans do: go to Le Hollandais and fasten your seatbelt for a remarkable meal.

AS

Prinses Irenestraat 19 - 1077 WT Amsterdam
T +31 20 644 0100 - www.restaurantas.nl
Lunch Tue.-Sun. 12.00-14.30, dinner Mon.-Sun. 18.30-23.00

A sign by the restaurant announces: 'Beware! Quicksands'. What? Quicksands? Here in Amsterdam? Yes, really! As is located next to Beatrix Park in the Zuidas business district between the Amstel and Schinkel rivers. This Financial Mile has fortunately kept some green areas around important office buildings.

Steak tartare

subtly modified version, very close to nature

The restaurant is established in the former St. Nicolaas chapel with a simple although eye-catching interior. It is a combination of 'table d'hôte' and individual tables that all seem to start from the center of the restaurant.

As features cuisine in its purest form. The passionate chef, Luuk Langendijk, very respectfully applies the concept that one must die to let the other live. His interesting creations are mostly determined by nature and every change of season or weather, even very subtle, is reflected on the menu.

One of my all-time favorites is steak tartare or filet américain préparé. What I find striking in this dish is the contrast between a warm, crunchy component, and the cold 'filet américain', or raw ground beef. I find it an amazing combination and one of the few dishes where temperature is almost used as seasoning.

Steak tartare is a dish served worldwide. Most often it is made of very lean, marinated beef or horse meat; the meat must be lean because in raw meat fat is not very tasty and gives a less pleasant feel in the mouth.

The version as we know it today appeared early in the 20th century in Paris restaurants, and was called 'beefsteak à l'américaine', American-style beefsteak; it was topped with a raw egg yolk. The dish became culinary history in 1903 when famous chef Escoffier included it in his cookbook titled *Le Guide Culinaire*. For the purists among us: there was no mention of raw egg yolk, but he did talk about tartare. Escoffier was stubborn.

In the 1938 edition of *Larousse gastronomique*, Escoffier's recipe has been modified and does include the raw egg yolk.

The tartare prepared in As is a very subtly modified version, very close to nature, like everything here.

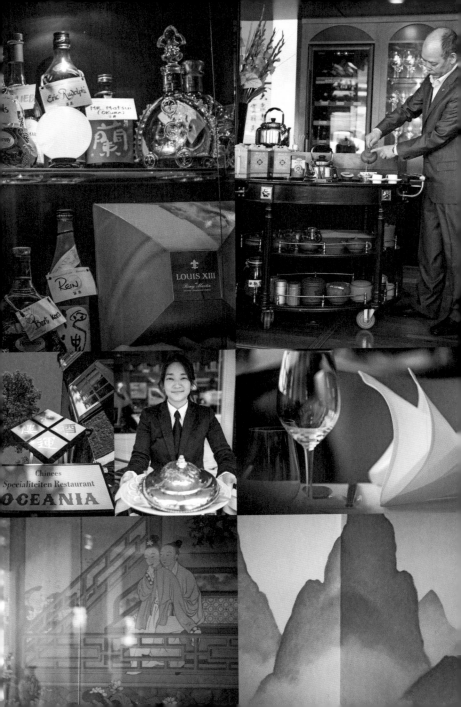

OCEANIA

Scheldestraat 77 - 1078 GH Amsterdam
T +31 20 673 8907 - www.restaurantoceania.nl
Mon.-Sun. 12.00-22.00

Geoffrey Chan, the driving force and manager of this very charming restaurant in the Rivierenbuurt, is the best cultural ambassador China could
ever hope for. He is a proud man, obviously very proud of his country of
origin. His restaurant is a natural expression of this pride.

Steamed oysters with black soybeans and spring onions

Coquilles St. Jacques (scallops) steamed with ginger and spring onions

Zeeland mussels with black bean sauce

It specializes in traditional Chinese dishes, mostly based on fish and seafood. I always thought that the best way to eat oysters was raw and pure, and I was often shocked to see, in most French seafood restaurants, people soaking their oysters in vinegar before covering them with black pepper. This was not lost to me. However, the first time I sampled oysters, steamed with black soybeans and spring onions, I had to revise my opinion.

In Chinese cuisine, you are very seldom served something raw or even cold to eat; consequently, oysters and seafood are generally prepared and cooked.

Black beans and black bean sauce have a thick texture and earthly touch that is definitely very close to that of some mushrooms. Therefore, many combinations are possible with all sorts of other ingredients. Black beans are also very popular in vegetarian dishes.

The combination of super fresh seafood with black beans and its preparation is an undisputed true hit.

I have a deep admiration for people like Geoffrey Chan, who runs much more than a restaurant. His deeply imbedded love and respect for all aspects of Chinese culture are endearing and utterly compelling. I have great admiration for this edifying culture that unfortunately sometimes strays away to a trivial consumption society. This is not the case when you hear Geoffrey talk. It is a true pleasure to chat with this man about China while he lets you taste one of the greatest Chinese delicacies: tea. In his restaurant, as in my heart, Chinese tea has a special place; it is prepared for you at your table in a very traditional way. Geoffrey will gladly guide you through his phenomenal tea menu to help you find your favorite one.

Blijf Gezond
Zeker weten?
Blijf Dan
Onze
Zuurwaren
Eten!

Hou de
Zon zij

DE LEEUW ZUURWAREN

Vrijheidslaan 78 - 1078 PP Amsterdam
T +31 20 662 8258 - www.deleeuwzuur.nl
Thu.-Fri. 09.00-18.00, Sun. 09.00-18.00

The Rivierenbuurt still has many hidden treasures. Since 1850, the De
Leeuw family has been making traditional Amsterdam-Yiddish pickles.
Fred de Leeuw and his wife Monique attach enormous value to fostering
and maintaining tradition.

Pickled herring

They still make the most delicious yellow cucumbers, pickle brines, Amsterdam onions, pickled herring....

Great-grandfather Isaac De Leeuw had a successful formula that is still used today. In those days, Isaak had developed his own pickle recipe, and pulled his cart along the Rivierenbuurt houses. The De Leeuw family only opened a fixed shop in 1970. Traditionally, Jews were not part of the well-off society in the Rivierenbuurt and De Leeuw provided affordable and long-life food that was also delicious.

This shop does not have a scale. Everything here is measured by the scoopful, by feel, and not by exact weight. It has been like this since the beginning, and probably always will be.

In the shop there is always a unique atmosphere, a sort of happy chaos. The tall jars containing colorful pickles seem very tempting. Isaac De Leeuw and Vincent Van Gogh knew each other well and from numerous writings of Vincent, it is clear that the master painter borrowed some of his colors from the green-yellow in Isaac's Amsterdam onions, pickles and cucumbers and from the robin-red of red cabbage in wine vinegar.

It is almost impossible to pass by this shop without stopping. In addition to pickle jars, you will find the very best pickled herring you will ever taste, along with a very traditional dish: pickled herring, baked and finished with pickles and herbs.

A national monument disguised as a shop!

HORNO LA MARIA

Vechtstraat 79 - 1079 JB Amsterdam
T +31 20 644 0712 - www.hornolamaria.com
Wed.-Sat. 18.00-22.30

Just steps away from the iconic and influential Floris and Diny and their
'Pasteibakkerij', you will find this über-cosy living room restaurant, Horno
La Maria. Step inside to the world of Rohan Grose, a young woman who
definitely knows what she wants.

Local suckling lamb, lemon beans from Lutjewinkel

A lot of ink is wasted to describe simplicity and authenticity when it comes to restaurants or food. For me, it seems authenticity is a place where people are where they seem to belong, where you see people who know what they want and who are able to make it. No tricks up their sleeve, just plain and simple, but oh so right. They do not try to impress you with big concepts or stories, they don't want to do it like it should be, no. They just do it the way they want, whether you like it or not. They don't care. They seem to be cooking for themselves rather than for an audience. I also see this in great artists. They do not ask themselves whether you are going to like their work. And that is a very admirable quality.

It is the kind of feeling that is more an expression of personality than professional conviction; it is a rare quality and even more rare when it comes to restaurants. Rohan has this quality, this way of life, and Horno La Maria has it too.

This restaurant is screaming in silence: Welcome with a capital W. This hidden gem is frequented by locals since it is set in an unexpected part of town. The Rivierenbuurt isn't really known for its fashionable, hipster-driven shops and restaurants. There used to be an important Jewish community here until WWII.

At first glance, there seems to be something missing in this restaurant: a kitchen. That's where the name of the restaurant starts making sense. You see a seriously sized white oven set on the edge of a bright dining room with an eclectic mix of chairs and tables of various sizes. If you look closely, you will notice that Rohan has a remarkable eye for detail. Tables are dressed with the essentials: a good knife, napkins and quality wine glasses. The wine list is vin nature only, not because it is trendy, but because that is how Rohan wants it to be.

Rohan spent quite some time in Argentina. There, she learned how to really work an oven so it is an all-in-one kitchen. For those who are wondering, she named her oven and her restaurant after her daughter. Her other source of inspiration, next to Argentina, is the pristine wildness of Sicily. She only buys food for one day of cooking, and at the end of the day, you can see that her mini-fridge is almost empty. Only what she sees at her favorite markets will find its way to your plate.

She is extremely calm when she is in her kitchen, or rather in front of her oven. She really knows her stuff and has great pleasure seeing that people are enjoying themselves in a simple manner. Good food and good wine at the dinner table. This place feels impressively right in every way.

Do yourself a favor: discover this place asap and experience just how authenticity is supposed to feel.

DE PASTEIBAKKERIJ

Hoendiepstraat 2 - 1079 LT Amsterdam
T +31 6 53475512 - www.depasteibakkerij.nl
Fri. 10.00-18.30, Sat. 10.00-16.30

I dare say that I absolutely love cold cuts; artisan charcuterie makers
are my heroes. I can't tell you how many thousands of kilometers I have
driven since learning that there was someone, somewhere, who made a
fantastic pâté, a divine wurst, or an insanely delicious terrine.

House-made cold cuts

Likewise, I have no idea how many kilometers of sausage and kilos of these unique pâtés I have already devoured.

One day I entered a small, unassuming deli. You know, somewhat messy, happily chaotic, accounting books tucked away in a closet, the inevitable picture of the noblest farm animal, the pig, and where every piece in the meat counter seems to scream: 'Eat me, I am even tastier than my neighbor'. Joyful sun rays give this little place an even greater feel of vacation. And of course, the owners have a glass of wine within reach! Then comes that magic moment, with the same tension a conductor tries to create in the nanosecond of silence before the first notes of Beethoven's Fifth Symphony. That magic moment arises when a slice of pâté is cut and your palate receives a bite of it. This first bite is enough for you to know that here, cold cuts are serious business. This pâté makes you suddenly very still and emotional. Everything about it is perfect: the firmness, the glorious coarse texture, the perfect seasoning. Am I dreaming? No! The slice of blood sausage is also disarmingly pure. This is no place for amateurs; this is a place of craftsmanship at the highest level. If the 'tête pressée', a terrine of pressed pig's head, was a painting, this version would surely be displayed in the Rijksmuseum in Amsterdam. I had landed in the deli Walhalla, and by chance, it is located in the Amsterdam Rivierenbuurt.

Diny Schouten and Floris Brester, both former food writers, realized that the specialties they enjoyed writing about were slowly but surely disappearing from the Dutch landscape. Since they both had a passion for cold cuts, they found their mission, their mantra. However, to make charcuterie, you need a little perversion. To be really good at it, you must make it often so as to refine and improve the taste and texture. This is why they found it necessary to start a small business.

They begin every week almost like conspirators, developing their repertoire of terrines and pâtés and people can buy these glorious delights on Fridays and Saturdays. There is also a table where you can sample their creations. Another magnificent finding is their Schiphol goose rillettes. The airport wants to get rid of these birds; here, the meat goes through a 20-hour cooking process, to be transformed into the best, purest rillettes ever. Isn't it nice that meat nobody wants can be changed into a delicious product?

Many people talk about 'nose to tail', but in this shop the motto is actually applied. There is something powerful in people who are able to produce something noble from apparently worthless things such as driftwood, water, or pig snout.

This place displays a rare level of purism and craftsmanship. Don't you even think of coming to Amsterdam without visiting this ode to taste!

GASTROBAR INDONESIA

Amstelzijde 51 - 1184 TZ Amstelveen
T + 31 20 496 1943 - www.rongastrobarindonesia.nl
Open daily, lunch 12.00-14.30, dinner 17.30-22.30

Ron Blaauw is a world-famous chef in Amsterdam. Indonesia, a former Dutch colony, has a very specific cuisine, much appreciated by the Dutch.

Refined Indonesian fare

To many Dutch people, eating Indonesian means getting in touch with their past. But unfortunately, in most cases, the glorious Indo food has been reduced to boring micro-waved fast food eaten on the couch while watching TV on a Sunday night.

Ron Blaauw's take on Indo food is quite different. It is about glorifying the rich traditional food of this beautiful archipelago. He hired a real local chef with heaps of talent to assure the authenticity of the dishes. Java-born Agus Hermawan inherited his passion for cooking from his mother, who taught him everything he knows. He came to Holland some 20 years ago to cook. His talent was recognised by the Indonesian Ministry of Tourism, which made him an official Ambassador for the gastronomical heritage of his country. This is certainly something

to be very proud of, and Agus himself considers it a real honour.

The restaurant is in a really beautiful setting in the gorgeous village of Ouderkerk aan de Amstel, right on the banks of the river as it meanders through the meadows. The menu offers the best Indonesian classics. What's surprising is that you can choose from the small-bites menu, which is divided into two parts. One part is the traditional culinary view of chef Agus, the other part is inspired by Ron Blaauw's vision and includes a wide selection of Indo dishes. This Indonesian restaurant stands out in all respects; it is a contemporary place that could easily blend into any other major city in the world. Oh, and if you're considering renting a boat to sail down the beautiful Amstel river, they have some takeaway specials.

ADDITIONAL EATERIES
SOUTH

**TUNES RESTAURANT
& BAR BY SCHILO** - €€€€
Van Baerlestraat 27
1071 AN Amsterdam
T +31 20 570 0000
▸ www.conservatoriumhotel.com

CHANG-I - €€€€
Jan Willem Brouwersstraat 7
1071 LH Amsterdam
T +31 20 470 1700
▸ www.chang-i.nl

EN PLUCHE - €€€
Ruysdaelstraat 48
1071 XE Amsterdam
T +31 20 471 4695
▸ www.enpluche.nl

LE GARAGE - €€€€
Ruysdaelstraat 54-56
1071 XE Amsterdam
T +31 20 679 7176
▸ www.restaurantlegarage.nl

THE FAT DOG - €€
Ruysdaelkade 251
1072 AX Amsterdam
T +31 20 221 6249
▸ www.thefatdog.nl

ALBINA - €€
Albert Cuypstraat 69
1072 CN Amsterdam
T +31 20 675 5135

THE BUTCHER - €
Albert Cuypstraat 129
1072 CS Amsterdam
T +31 20 470 7875
▸ www.the-butcher.com

SIR HUMMUS - €
Van der Helstplein 2
1072 PH Amsterdam
T +31 20 664 7055
▸ www.sirhummus.nl

UMENO - €€€
Agamemnonstraat 27
1076 LP Amsterdam
T +31 20 676 6089
▸ www.umeno.nl

THE ROAST ROOM - €€€€
Europaplein 2
1078 GZ Amsterdam
T +31 20 723 9614
▸ www.theroastroom.nl

HAKATA SENPACHI - €€€
Wielingenstraat 16
1078 KK Amsterdam
T +31 20 662 5823
▸ www.hakatasenpachi.com

HALVEMAAN - €€€€
Van Leijenberghlaan 320
1082 DD Amsterdam
T +31 20 644 0348
▸ www.restauranthalvemaan.nl

KHAN - €€
Nederhoven 9
1083 AM Amsterdam
T +31 20 646 3722

TJIN'S - €€€€
Eerste van der Helststraat 64
1072 NZ Amsterdam
T +31 20 671 7708

BRANDT & LEVIE

Archangelkade 9 - 1013 BE Amsterdam
T +31 88 044 2100 - www.brandtenlevie.nl
Mon.-Fri. 10.00-18.00, Sat. 09.00-17.30

The Gods of salami have evolved. Brandt&Levie started out by renting a butcher shop during the night to try and make salami.

Hot and other Dogs

Their initial production was so small that they knew where every salami went and who ate it. Soon they had a cult following because their quality was, and still is, amongst Europe's finest. Imagine tasting this and then being told that it is made in Amsterdam. You'll be staring in disbelief and asking where the hidden camera is.

Three friends (and chefs), Jiri, Geert and Samuel, pursued one dream: to create the perfect sausage. While sitting in the waiting room to the office of Carlo Petrini, founder of Slow Food, they received a big surprise. Petrini walked out of his office enthusiastically, eager to meet the three penniless Jewish boys who wanted to dedicate their lives to making pork sausages and cold cuts. Petrini and Dario Cecchini became their mentors and are still friends.

The secret behind their success is very simple: free-range Dutch pigs, delivered as whole carcasses and cut into pieces by highly qualified butchers.

Every impurity and every tendon has to be removed in order to make the best final product. Everything is used; this is a no-waste company. They even make soap from the fat surrounding the kidneys.

Brandt&Levie have the vision and the craftmanship to produce really amazing food. Try the delicately smoked ham, the coppa, the pulled pork, the paté, and of course, the hotdogs. The three friends have reinstated the hotdog as a worthy, tasteful snack. They moved to this small industrial atelier, hoping to give people an insight into how they work and to provide transparency. So they reproduced a small vintage-looking butcher's shop with a large window to the atelier where carcasses are cut up. There you can buy their products and enjoy a sandwich or hotdog. The sandwich menu changes daily.

As one of the icons of the new high-quality movements in Dutch gastronomy, Brandt&Levie is an ambassador and preacher of quality.

MOS

IJdok 185 - 1013 MM Amsterdam
T + 31 20 638 0866 - www.mosamsterdam.nl
Mon.-Fri. 12.00-15.00, 18.00 till late night, Sat. 18.00 till late night

The beautiful views of 't IJ have of course always been there,
but it seems as though they've only recently been discovered. While restaurants offering their guests views of 't IJ used to be rare, lately there has
been a marked increase in such restaurants.

Salad of Bomba rice with cockles & mussels, avocado, apple and a vinaigrette with anchovy and chorizo.

The name of this place is quite the opposite of what it suggests. The high ceiling gives the restaurant a comfortable, cosy, and luxurious ambience. Through the tall windows you have a sweeping view from Central Station to the lights at NDSM island. The vibe is chic and bustling and really evokes the Marrakech-meets-Paris atmosphere it aims for. The large space is divided into smaller intimate spaces.

The cuisine is French-international and the seasons dictate the menu. The chef, Egon Van Hoof, used to run the kitchen at the two-Michelin-star Aan de Poel. This naturally raises expectations, but you will not be disappointed. Egon's food is brilliant. He has the ability to turn his dishes into small works of art without destroying the dishes' essentials themselves.

Mos offers a true dining experience, especially if you fully immerse yourself in the vibe of this beautiful place. And although it is only 500 m away from Central station, if you decide to come by car, call ahead so you can park in the nearby public car park.

FOODHALLEN

Bellamyplein 51 - 1053 AT Amsterdam
www.foodhallen.nl
Sun.-Wed. 11.00-23.30, Thu.-Sat. 11.00-01.00

In many major European cities, indoor food markets are a big success.
Amsterdam is finally among those cities where you can wander around a
bustling market and fulfill all your food cravings.
The Foodhallen are finally open!

Oon Iberico
€ 5

Cono Iberico
"Cebo"
€ 4

Cono Iberico
Bellota
€ 6

BELGIAN FRIES ~

Pink Flaming

RAMONES

KANDINSKY
TRY 4
DIFFERENT

funky

HOMEMADE
> HOTDOGS <

ONLY EAT HOTDOGS ON TWO
OCCASIONS, WHEN IT'S MY
BIRTHDAY AND WHEN IT'S NOT!

The
BUTCHER
AMSTERDAM

Local vendors

Rakish Gangapersad, Chong Chu, Tsibo Lin and Zing-kyn Cheung were walking around the Mercado de San Miguel in Madrid when they came up with the brilliant idea of creating an indoor market in their hometown, Amsterdam. And so they did!

I went there a few days after it opened and it was love at first sight. The building is a former tram shed, transformed into foodie heaven. I joined Hari Shetty, the chef at Izakaya and Momo, who said that my craving for real kebab would soon be fulfilled. He served me a brilliant tasty chicken tikka kebab at Shirkhan while they were still working on the last stalls, but everything was up and running.

The more than twenty food stalls at the Foodhallen have one thing in common:

an unbelievable dedication to quality. To be a foodie is evidently considered hereditary. There is nothing better than a place under one roof where you can nibble at a multitude of food cultures. What's your craving for tonight? Viet View's rolls, or Meneer Temaki's sushi-rolls? Or, do you fancy some of Shirkhan's kebab rather than some Smokey Goodness from the Rough Kitchen? It must be said that diversity has played a huge part in the range of food offered here at the Foodhallen.

Here, I always feel like Alice in Foodie-Wonderland. For me, the Foodhallen is the ideal brunch or aperitif stroll. The atmosphere is always very pleasant, and the food is stunning and so savoury. This is rapidly becoming one of the best and most visited attractions in Amsterdam.

BEYROUTH

Kinkerstraat 18 - 1053 DV Amsterdam
T + 31 20 616 0635 - www.restaurantbeyrouth.online
Open daily 17.00-23.00

Beyrouth is one of those under-the-radar restaurants where only locals
go. It's nothing fancy, but you get the best Lebanese fare in the city.

Mezze

↓

Sit round a table and share.

Lebanese cuisine is one of the world's top cuisines and many of the dishes are the basis of what we call Mediterranean cuisine. Lebanese dishes excel in their excellent use of olive oil, lemon, and a perfect balance of herbs and spices. These and hummus, perfect grilled, are the things that Lebanese chefs have taught the rest of the world. This restaurant is the perfect setting for a mezze. People are incredibly friendly and make you feel at home. Beyrouth is simple and small, but don't let that scare you.

The best way to discover the generosity of the Lebanese and their cuisine is to try a mezze. Mezze is for the Lebanese what tapas are for the Spanish and antipasto for the Italians: a selection of small plates offering typical dishes to share, both cold and hot. A Lebanese mezze is usually more generous than in other Mediterranean countries and you get a taste of what the chef does best. One of the best ways to let the day or evening gently roll by is to sit round a table and share a mezze. And don't forget, in Lebanon it is considered impolite to finish everything on your plate.

DE SCHOOL/RESTAURANT DS

Doctor Jan van Breemenstraat 1 - 1056 AB Amsterdam
T +31 20 737 3197 - www.deschoolamsterdam.nl
Tue.-Sat. 18.00-22.00

De School, Amsterdam's new nightlife venue, is a huge sixties-style school buillding that houses a nightclub, a restaurant, a cultural complex, and offices all under one roof.

7 course tasting menu

The idea behind De School, which holds a round-the-clock licence, was to create a city within a city that would accommodate cultural events, concerts, workshops, and a full bar and restaurant, which is why it is often referred to as a cultural institution. The owners used to own Trouw, a legendary nightclub in Amsterdam, and thanks to their audacious programming, Amsterdam is back on the map of international clubbing.

When Trouw closed down, Amsterdammers were in shock, but the Trouw team worked more than a year to create a worthy successor, and they succeeded. De School has more possibilities than Trouw: it has gardens, a gym, a bar, a café, a concert hall, a club and, of course, restaurant DS.

The old garage shop where students learned how to repair cars was transformed into this gem of a restaurant, whose original industrial function offers a striking contrast to the candlelit intimate dinner tables with white linen tablecloths. No longer just a hangout for kids, Restaurant DS attracts a high-end clientele who can choose from three to seven courses of delicious, high-quality seasonal products.

After you eat here, head for the club with its underground vibe. It is set in an old garage with a low ceiling that creates a special atmosphere. Here you can really lose yourself in the live music. There are two DJs per night who have no fixed schedules.

PARTISAN

Admiraal de Ruijterweg 79 - 1057 JZ Amsterdam
T +31 20 846 2361 - www.cafepartisan.nl
Mon.-Thu. 17.00-01.00, Fri. 17.00-03.00, Sat. 12.30-03.00, Sun. 12.30-01.00

Arjan Teerink, Daan Bonsen, Leonardo Beloni, and Sander Ravesloot
have teamed up once again to open this place in a part
of town called De Baarsjes.

Slowly braised beef Rib

They already jointly own Panache and have turned it into a success thanks to their teamwork. Partisan is their own concept of a café, where wine and great food are the epicentre of attention.

The dishes are without unnecessary blah blah and are built in a classical way. Each dish contains a maximum of five ingredients that don't compete for attention but rather evoke harmony. There is a slight focus on pork, game, and poultry.

The overall style and vibe of this place is light and fresh. According to Teerink,

this is due to the combination of two formats, where you can either come in for dinner or just pop in for drinks and small bites. The owners really want to give guests the freedom to drop by for classy cocktails, small bites, shared plates, or a range of wines that suit all budgets and styles.

Lunch is only offered on weekends. Partisan is a full-blown neighbourhood bar where you can meet for drinks, dinner, and pretty much everything in between. Partisan is sure to find a place in your heart.

We werken

HELE DIE

dus son

VANG JE

ADDITIONAL EATERIES
WEST

PENDERGAST - €€€
Groen van Prinstererstraat 14
1051 EG Amsterdam
T +31 20 845 8507
▶ **www.pendergast.nl**

GRACELAND BBQ - €€€
Jan van Galenstraat 8
1051 KM Amsterdam
T +31 20 723 1760
▶ **www.gracelandbbq.com**

MORGAN & MEES - €€€
Tweede Hugo de Grootstraat 2
1052 LC Amsterdam
T +31 20 233 4930
▶ **www.morganandmees.com**

CHAMPAGNERIA FIVE BROTHERS FAT - €€€
De Clercqstraat 56
1052 NH Amsterdam
T +31 20 77 60 770
▶ **www.fivebrothersfat.nl**

MIJNHEER DE WIT HEEFT HONGER - €€€
Witte de Withstraat 10
1057 XV Amsterdam
T +31 20 737 3184
▶ **www.meneerdewitheefthonger.nl**

ALPHABETICAL INDEX

Kaagman en Kortekas
La Fiorita
Rest Vermeer
Rest Marius

Colophon

www.lannoo.com
Register on our website to regularly receive our newsletter
with new publications as well as exclusive offers.

Texts: Luc Hoornaert
Photography: Kris Vlegels, except for the pictures of Librije's zusje
Translation: Marguerite Storm
Editing: Bracha De Man
Book design: Grietje Uytdenhouwen
Cover design & illustrations: Emma Thyssen

If you have any questions or remarks, do not hesitate to contact our
editorial team: redactiekunstenstijl@lannoo.com.

© Lannoo Publishers, 2017
ISBN: 978 94 014 4762 1
Registration of copyright: D/2017/45/538
NUR: 440/504